KIDS <u>CAN</u> WRITE!

A BASIC MIDDLE SCHOOL WRITING PROGRAM
ILLUSTRATED WITH STUDENT SAMPLES FROM 1961-1981

by

Chuck Dowdle

Mary K.,

Peace + Joy!

Chuck Dowdle

RED LEAD PRESS
PITTSBURGH, PENNSYLVANIA 15222

ISBN: 978-0-8059-8389-0
Library of Congress Control Number: 2006935735
Printed in the United States of America

First Printing

For more information or to order additional books, please contact:
Red Lead Press
701 Smithfield Street
Third Floor
Pittsburgh, Pennsylvania 15222
U.S.A.
1-800-834-1803
www.redleadbooks.com

Acknowledgments

I owe many thanks to a number of people whose work has made it possible for this book to become a reality.

First, I owe a special thanks to my wife, Marty, who did all of the typing and shared the editing process of the student samples with me. She was a constant source of encouragement and labored right alongside me until the book was completed.

Second, I should like to thank all of my students. They are the kids who searched their heads and hearts for something worthwhile to say. They are the ones who had the skill and the courage to willingly share their experiences with the rest of the world. I love them and respect them.

Lastly, I'd like to thank James Moffett for developing a new rationale for an English curriculum. His work helped synthesize the total language arts program for me, and his thinking fired my mind and inspired me to experiment with my junior high students.

Thanks to all of you for the part you played in helping make this book possible.

Chuck Dowdle
Teacher of English
Santa Rosa, California 95405
January, 1983

Preface

The purpose of this book is to provide an easy, convenient to teach, basic writing program for middle school students. By examining student-written examples for each of the sequenced writing assignments, student writers are able to advance at their own pace without the need for extensive explanations. The students learn by "hands on" experience, imitating models written by students like themselves. The accomplishment of each assignment with the student samples as incentives moves the student writers through a series of writing successes and a constructive learning program.

Each of the writing assignments was usually preceded by a listening-speaking exercise: improvisations, conversations, dictations, small group and whole class discussions, speeches, debates, etc. Also, review of the forms of writing took place often to help students gain a better understanding and mastery of the total writing program.

Introduction

Kids! You can write! Don't ever let anyone tell you otherwise! You've been thinking, feeling, listening, and speaking ever since you were toddlers. You've done exciting things, been to fun places, and have met interesting people. You've had many rich experiences about which to write, so why not share them with others. That's what this book is all about, showing you how to get what's already in you, out of you, so it can be shared with others. That's the purpose of language, to share our experiences.

Others will benefit by learning from what you write just as I hope you will benefit by learning from what my former junior high school students from Santa Rosa, California have written and been willing to share with you.

I hope you find the following assignments so easy to understand and the student-written samples so enjoyable to read that you will be encouraged and eager to write the assignments yourselves.

Contents

Assignment 1 - Monologues

Do you remember a time when you were by yourself and you were thinking about something important that was going to happen or that had just happened? That thinking is called an **INTERIOR MONO-LOGUE**. If you were to speak out that thinking into a tape recorder, you would have a permanent impression of it. Think of one of those very important moments in your life when you did some extremely serious thinking and try to record that thinking on paper in writing. Try to recapture the exact wording of your thinking as accurately as possible, and especially try to recapture the feeling you had. Use the first person pronoun - I.

"First Day at Junior High"

I sure hope my hair turns out well. Yuck! I hate it! I wonder what everyone's wearing today. I bet Tammy is wearing her new sweater.

I wonder what all the people are like at Rincon. Will they hate me? Will I have friends? I get scared when I even think about it.

Gosh, switching classes six times! I hope I'll be able to keep up. I hear you don't get very much time, and even if you're a minute late, you get a tardy.

Well, this is it. I'm on my way to school. I have the worst butterflies in my stomach! I'm so nervous! I hope I see someone I know.

So far, so good. Oh, there's Jennifer. Now if I can only get my locker open. Shoot! You stupid locker! I can't get it open! How embarrassing. Is everybody staring at me? I hope not. I'll totally die!

Gosh, the bell! I'd better hurry. Oh, shut the locker. Now don't be stupid, Kristen. Is this it? Yes, this is the classroom, 26. Oh, the teacher doesn't look that mean. I can already tell this is going to be a great year at Rincon Valley Junior High.

Kristen Daniels
Seventh Grade - 1981

For your second monologue, try to think of one of those times when you were with one or more persons, but you did all the talking. It's called a DRAMATIC MONOLOGUE. No one interrupts you. You just go on and on. Usually, you're very excited, you have a lot to tell the person or people you're with, and you just have to get it all out at once. Try to recall the exact wording of what you said as you write it.

"My First Week at R.V.J.H.S."

My first week at Rincon Valley Junior High School was almost the best week of my life! I just love it! You should see it! It's so big! There are so many classes! But after the first two or three days you catch on real easy. I'm not late to any of my classes any more. And I can open my locker real easy now.

And the snack bar is a blast! It's real neat. At nutrition break and lunch they play neat music. And they have some great stuff to eat. I hope I get to work at the snack bar some day.

And you know what? The eighth and ninth graders don't pick on me at all. In fact, most of them are really nice. They help you find your classes, and they help you get your lockers open. They also help you on almost anything else you can think of.

And my teachers are really nice, too. I was so afraid I'd have a lot of mean teachers, but every single one of them is pretty nice. They help you when you need help, and they aren't any stricter than my teachers were at Binkley. I like every single one of them. I've got : Mr. Dowdle, English, first period; Mrs. King-Claye, Gym, second period; Mr. Bennett, Health, third period; Mrs. Hagemann, Geography, fourth period; Mr. Farmiloe, Math, fifth period; and Mr. Schultz, Drama, sixth period.

I was almost sad when Friday came because I loved school so much. And I couldn't wait for Monday to come. Friday was a good day. I got my gym clothes stenciled, and got my gym locker.

My favorite teacher is Mr. Bennett. He's my health teacher. He's really funny, and he's super nice. I wish I had gotten reading first, though. I just love reading. It's my favorite hobby.

2

You wouldn't believe how many new friends I've met. I didn't get any classes with Katrina, my best friend, but I see her at snack break and at lunch. Once in a while I'll see her while we're changing classes.

And they also have pretty good food for hot lunch. I wish it didn't cost so much, though. My mom can't afford it. But, that's life.

So, all in all, I love it at R.V.J.H. I never imagined that seventh grade could be this great. My first week at R.V.J.H. was GREAT!

Cindy Maynard
Seventh Grade - 1981

Assignment 2 - Dialogues

Dialogue is simply conversation between two or more people. Pick any situation. No quotation marks are needed. However, you must identify who said what. Material for this assignment can be found anywhere people have conversations: in families, at school, with friends, etc. Record the conversation as accurately as you remember it. It might even help if you initiate a conversation with the thought in mind of putting it in writing immediately after it's finished. Also, you may want to try being a silent observer, listening to a conversation between two or more persons, and then trying to accurately record it in writing.

"Phone Call"

Carol: Hello, Judy?

Judy: Oh, hi Carol!

Carol: How's life with you?

Judy: I'm doing great! How about you?

Carol: I'm fine. We got a new puppy.

Judy: Really? What kind?

Carol: It's kind of hard to tell.

Judy: So, it's a mutt?

Carol: I guess that's what you'd call it.

Judy: What did you name it?

Carol: We haven't thought of a good name yet.

Judy: Oh, I see. How about "Rover"?

Carol: No. Too plain.

Judy: Fifi?

Carol: No. Too odd-ballish.

Judy: Well, what color is it?

Carol: A whole bunch of colors.

Judy: Uh, let's see . . .

Carol: Hard to find a name, huh?

Judy: Really. How about Mopsy?

Carol: Mopsy!

Judy: Well . . .

Carol: Can I wipe my floor with it, too?

Judy: I was just trying to give you a suggestion.

Carol: I know. I was just kidding.

Judy: O.K.

Carol: I think we should just call it "Rover".

Judy: Really. Save yourself trouble.

Kelly Boyce
Eighth Grade - 1981

"The Stupid Lamp"

Mom: Steve! Did you break this lamp?

Steve: (Oh, no! I'm going to be in so much trouble.) Yes, Mom. I did.

Mom: Steve, how could you! That cost me $120! When your father comes home, he'll go through the roof!

Steve: (I knew she would say that. She always gets Dad on me.) Mom, I'm really sorry! I didn't mean to do it.

Mom: Yes, that's what you always say. I know you didn't mean it, but we have to put a stop to it. Do you understand?

Steve: Yes.

Mom: Well, what do you think we should do about it?

Steve: I don't know.

Mom: Well, here's the broom. Clean it up.

Steve: I am sorry, Mom. (I hope she leaves now. I said I was sorry.)

Mom: Now go to your room for an hour and close your door.

Steve: (I sure hope it's all over now.) O.K.

Mom: Never say "O.K." or "ya." Always say, "yes."

Steve: Yes, Mom. (I hope I don't have to pay for the lamp. I don't have much money. That stupid lamp!)

Mom: Steve, come up here!

Steve: Yes.

Mom" Look at my foot! It's cut because I stepped on some of the glass you were suppose to have cleaned up. Now clean the rest up!

Steve: (I wish she wouldn't get so mad and stay cooler like my friends' moms do.) O.K., I mean, yes, Mom.

Steve Sorenson
Seventh Grade - 1981

Assignment 3 - Short Plays

Your daily life is filled with short plays. <u>People</u> in <u>action</u> and <u>talking</u> to one another is the stuff short plays are made of. The fancy names are: character, plot, and dialogue. Begin this assignment by thinking about an interesting happening in your life. Now divide that happening into <u>events</u> or <u>scenes</u>. Usually, a new scene begins when there's an important change in the action, time, or place. When you write a short play, you tell not only what a character says, but also <u>how</u> he says it. You tell <u>where</u> the characters move and <u>how</u> they move. Also, you briefly describe what's happening, where and when, in each scene before the speaking and action begin. You, the writer, are in total control of what the actors do and say when you write a short play. Have some fun by trying to recapture an interesting experience involving a number of people! Your <u>short play</u> must necessarily occur over a longer period of time than a simple conversation in order to be called a <u>short play</u>. Now is the time to recreate that favorite experience you always enjoy telling others.

"Camping"

Characters:
Father - frustrated, typical father
Mom - a mother who is rapidly growing tired of camping
Floyd - typical ten year old "pain in the neck brother
Kim - ordinary, run-of-the-mill, slightly obnoxious, 12 year old
Oliver - Siamese cat
Mia - Beagle dog, slightly obese

7

Scene I

This scene takes place in the upper bunk of a camper. A soft, mellow light allows a dark form entangled in a sleeping bag to come into view. It's Kim. She is desperately trying to finish a good book, but is failing. The camper is on the back of a moving pickup. There is a tremendous rocking motion in the bunk, and the sound of wind makes it apparent that it is storming outside. Kim is rapidly getting sick.

Kim: (In a monotonous voice) I am getting sick; I am getting sick; I am getting sick.

Oliver: Meow!

Kim: Well sung, dear sir, but we passed the last bathroom yay many miles ago.

(Camper grinds to a stop, and after a pause, the back door is flung open.)

Mom: Kim, come on down from there.

Kim: What for?

Mom: We're afraid the camper is going to blow over!

Kim: Oh! Well, I can't leave the animals back here.

Mom: All right! Grab 'em, but hurry it up!

Kim: (Scrambling around a few moments) Mom, Oliver has dug himself into the bookshelf, and I can't pry him loose.

Mom: Well, forget him and get the beagle.

Kim: Mother! ! !

Mom: In case you hadn't noticed, it is below zero out here, and I am rapidly turning blue!

Kim: (Exultantly) I got him!! (She comes down out of the camper, rather slowly and painfully, with a cat and a beagle entwined about her person. The wind is ferocious, and she is almost blown off her feet. Carefully, they return to the cab of the truck.)

Father:	What took you?
Mom:	It's a long story, and I'll tell ya as soon as my tongue unfreezes.
Kim:	Oliver needs a potty.
Lloyd:	I need a potty.
Father:	Damn it! !
Kim:	How long 'til we get to wherever we're going?
Father:	We are attempting to go to the south shore of Tahoe, but if this wind and other things (he casts a glance at Oliver) keep up, I'm not sure we'll ever make it.
Oliver:	Meeeeow!
Mia:	(Snoring happily) Z Z Z
Oliver:	Ahoahahah! !
Kim:	Oh, my god, Oliver went! !
Mom:	Watch your language.
Lloyd:	If he can go, why can't I?
Father:	Damn!
Mom:	Wait . . . . I have a Kleenex.

(They all hold their noses in disgust as ever-patient Mom scoops up the mess. There is a long sigh of relief when it is deposited out the window.)

Lloyd:	Mom, I can't hold it any longer. Stop the car.
Father:	Oh, damn! (Car grinds to a stop.)
Mom:	Well, get out and go.
Lloyd:	It looks awful cold.

Kim: And windy.

Mom: True.

Lloyd: And dark.

Mom: True.

Lloyd: I think I can hold it.

Father: (sigh)

Kim: How can you tell when the camper is going to blow off?

Father: You would hear a sharp snap, and we would go rolling over and over 'til we plunged to our deaths.

Lloyd: Daddy! (sharp snap)

Kim: Aaaah! (scream)

Father: Oh, no!

Mom: Heaven help us! (There is a long pause. Then there is a huge sigh of relief.)

Mia: (whimper)

Kim: I think . . .

Father: I know. Mia needs to go.

Kim: Right. Howdja guess? (truck stops)

Father: I'll walk her. (Mia wags happily.) (Father tramps up and down in the snow.) Please, Mia! Pretty please with a cherry on top! Oh, come on!

(5 minutes later)

Kim: What took ya?

Father: (dirty look)

Kim: Did she go?

Father: We stood there, and stood there, 'til finally . . .

Lloyd: What?

Father: I realized she wouldn't go.

Mom: Oh.

Scene II

Worn out and exhausted, they arrive at the campsite. Snow is abundant.

Kim: Snow!

Lloyd: Snow?

Mom: Snow . . .

Father: Snow.

Mia: Ahahah.

Mom: (sigh) I'll clean it up!

Scene III

This scene takes place in the camper. If the light had been on, you could have seen clothes washed and hung out to dry in various positions. Voices are coming from the darkness.

Father: <u>We</u> are out of gas.

Mom: (dryly) So I see.

Kim: We'll perish horribly in this frozen wilderness.

Father: You mean, we will get a little nippy in this home away from home, half a mile from the gambling capital of the world.

Kim: Spoilsport!

Lloyd:	Mama, I'm cold!
Father:	Now where the hell do ya get camper gas at night?
Mom:	My clothes won't dry.
Kim:	Like I said . . .
Father:	Never mind. (As he leaves the camper, he slips on some ice.)
Lloyd:	Daddy hath fallen!
Kim:	Hey, Lloyd, that's really cute, really cute.
Mom:	Are you hurt?
Father:	It only hurts when I snarl!
Kim:	It must hurt a lot of the time.
Father:	Cute, Kim, really cute.

Scene IV

They cautiously leave the camper in search of food.

Father:	Now, according to this map there should be a restaurant in that direction.
Kim:	"Forward and onward," as the noble Perry said.
Lloyd:	Bet he didn't!
Kim:	Did!
Lloyd:	Didn't!
Kim:	Did!
Lloyd:	Didn't!
Kim:	Did!

Mom: All right! Shut up! Be quiet!!

Kim: All right already.

(They proceed cautiously over ice and powdery snow. Lloyd decides to take a short-cut across a fluffy drift.)

Lloyd: Look at me! I'll get there first. Ooooooo!!!

Kim: (Careless tone) Lloyd's gone.

Father: He fell in a snow drift.

Mom: Lloyd! Lloyd!

Lloyd: (reappearing, groggy, in tears) I got snow down my mouth, and my eyes, and my nose, and my ears, and my pants.

Kim: I've heard of being one with nature, but this is ridiculous.

Mom: (admonishing tone) Kim!

Father: (after a few more steps) Well, here we are at the restaurant.

Kim: Civilization!

Lloyd: Food!

Mom: Warmth!

(They eat and return to the camper with a newly purchased sun lamp.)

Mom: Well, I certainly feel better now that I've eaten.

Father: Now, hopefully, we can warm up and unfreeze our underwear.

Lloyd: Yeah, boy!

Kim: Dumb, Lloyd, really dumb.

Mom: Straighten up, young lady! None of that smart talk now!

Kim: (dirty look)

Oliver: (sitting in a boot under the sun lamp) Maw.

Mia: (snores)

Scene V

Next morning, after eating breakfast, they head home. As they pull out . . .

Father: Glad that's over. Wow! What an experience! I'm sure nothing else could happen to us now. (He turns the corner, and suddenly there is a shriek of crumpling metal. The truck hit an ice spot and went merrily sliding into another car, leaving a dent in it.)

Father: Oh, crap!!

Mom: Well, I'll leave our address.

Kim: Goody, goody!

Mom: One more word out of you, young lady, and your T.V. privileges are restricted for a <u>week</u>. (They continue on.)

Father: Well, now I'm certain nothing more can happen to us.

Kim: Yeah.

Lloyd: Yeah.

Mom: Hmmm.

Oliver: Ahoahahah!!

(And so they fade into the horizon, accompanied by a fowl odor and muffled swearing and a . . .)

Lloyd: Daddy, I need to go, too.

Kim Haylock
Eighth Grade - 1970

Assignment 4 - Letters

Write a letter to an elected official like the President of the United States or to an important member of your family like your mom or dad. This is also a good time to write letters to friends and relatives who live a distance from you. Some of your classmates probably have pen pals. Ask them how they got them so you can write to pen pals, too.

Santa Rosa, California
May 10, 1972

Richard M. Nixon
President of the United States
The White House
Washington, D.C

Dear Mr. President:

I would like to inquire about your feelings concerning the draft. I am aware of the present draft system, and I was wondering what your thoughts were prior to the 1972 election.

Although the "lottery method" seems to be fair and equitable, I believe there are many boys entering the service reluctantly. I would like to believe that I am a good American and would defend my country if I were called to do so, but you must agree that many do not feel that way. Therefore, a way should be devised whereby those who do not wish to fight or kill are not required to serve. In your reply, please state your feelings on this matter, and what you propose to do if elected president in 1972.

Sincerely yours,

Jill Joyce
Eighth Grade - 1972

•   •   •

Santa Rosa, California
May 12, 1981

Ronald Regan
President of the United States
The White House
Washington, D.C

Dear President Regan:

There is a big problem that is bothering me. I'm sure it bothers everyone else, also. It is inflation. Inflation is extremely and ridiculously high. Gas prices are pathetic! By the time I get my license to drive, I won't be able to afford gas, let alone a car! I know you hear complaints about this from everyone, but I think it's time you did something about it. Please do your best!

Sincerely,

Kelly Boyce
Eighth Grade - 1981

•   •   •

Santa Rosa, California
April 19, 1981

Ronald Regan
President of the United States
The White House
Washington, D.C.

Dear President Regan:

I'm writing this letter to you to show my concern about your economic policies and the budget cuts you are making in many of the social programs made to support many of the people of this nation. I certainly support some of your cuts, but taking the money and putting it into military expenditures is a different matter. What you are doing, in fact, is taking money collected to support the nation and spending it on what inevitably will be used to destroy it.

I do understand that the strengthening of the military is important for our national security, but I do not believe that we should go to such an extent as to start an arms race. We already have enough nuclear warheads to destroy every Russian city 300 times. Isn't that enough?

Sincerely yours,

David Jager
Seventh Grade - 1981

•   •   •

4050 Wallace Road
Santa Rosa, CA 95404
October 1, 1981

The Honorable Don Sebastiani
Room 4177
State Capitol
Sacramento, CA 95814

Sir:

I have read the article in the newspaper titled "Federal Rules Eased on Transit for the Disabled." The United States has now made it so the handicapped of America can not ride the buses on the regular time schedule. Therefore, the handicapped now have to ride in a van.

I think the handicapped deserve to have public transportation. It is unfair to the handicapped to take away the wheelchair accessibility on buses. The handicapped need the bus transportation and the government's support. The handicapped are citizens of the United States and need our support. The United States has made it clear that all men in the country shall have equal rights. From my point of view, it is not working that way. The handicapped are getting something very important taken away from them, and that is our support.

The handicapped deserve the right to ride buses and ride anywhere in the United States, or at least in Santa Rosa.

The handicapped need the wheelchair accessibility; they need to ride on the regular time schedule; they need our support. They need all of these rights, but they don't need what we have in store for them.

I am concerned about the handicapped and hope you will be, too, and support them. Please take this letter into some consideration.

Sincerely,

Michael F. Kosta
Seventh Grade - 1981

•   •   •

Santa Rosa, California
May 31, 1978

Dear Plant Sitter (Mom),

While I'm gone on vacation, living it up, you will have the pleasure of watching over my plants. I think you'll enjoy getting to know them. They kind of grow on you after a while! I water them every Saturday, and I'd appreciate it if you could keep the same routine. You can use the jar that is on the cedar chest. You will have to fill the jar three or four times to water <u>all</u> the plants. There is also a bottle of plant food on the cedar chest. Put a full dropper of food in each full jar of water. After you have watered them, they like to take a shower. Just squirt them a few times with the sprayer. Any time you have a spare moment during the week, you can always go and spray them. They love it! Repeat this same routine on the next Saturday and the next and so on. Thank you very much for doing all of this.

Now for a few comments about each plant so you can get to know them better!

You once knew Mike, but he started dying on you. I took him from the garbage can and revived him. He might feel badly toward you for abandoning him the way you did, but don't let his attitude get you down. At the present time Mike isn't doing too well, and he might die on you. Don't feel too badly if he does because his time has come. He is "over the hill" and has lived a long, happy life. Treat him with extra care because he will be very moody. When and if he does pass on, the necessary

18

arrangements to take care of him have already been made. Be sensitive towards him!

Leroy is the healthy spider plant. Right now he is about to bring his first child into the world. Assuming you have never witnessed the birth of a baby spider plant, I will tell you what needs to be done. First of all, I'm sure you can see the skinny shoot with the beginnings of a baby in progress coming from Leroy's center. If a flower happens to appear near the new baby, don't panic! This is how Leroy shows his excitement over the new addition to the family. Leroy was just a baby himself when I started caring for him. He's come a long way since then! This is a very emotional time in his life, and he will often need your encouragement. Give it to him along with weekly watering. (Note: I'm sure Leroy can handle the birth on his own, so there is no need to call a doctor. He would prefer a natural childbirth!)

Alice is the very ugly Wandering Jew. She was raised from a single cutting and is growing like a weed. In fact, she looks like one, too! Alice is not very attractive and believes that looks aren't everything. She feels that the package you are in doesn't matter -- it's the feelings and love you have inside that count. Alice isn't too horribly exciting to talk to. I always thought she was a loner, afraid of others, but I guess I was wrong! The other plants told me that she might be having an affair with Leroy. Whatever you do, don't split them up. I want this relationship to grow! Keep them together.

The Fish Family plant is known as a "Moses-in-the-Cradle" in the plant world. Fish is the family name. The children are the smaller sprouts on the right side of the pot, and Mom and Dad are on the left. They're just an average family; the kids fight, Mom worries, and Dad loves to watch or listen to baseball games. This family, like most, all love each other. They have faced the fact that they are literally stuck together. Treat them as you would any family.

Tillie is the "Asparagus Fern." You also once knew her! She was turning yellow because you didn't give her enough light. She is now located in a well-lit spot and will soon turn back to her natural shade of green. Tillie and Mike have been through a lot together and are very close friends. She will be very upset if he dies. Keep her next to Mike at all times (unless he dies). If he does, you must break the news to her very carefully. She is a very sensitive plant and might consider suicide if he leaves her. Love her and be her friend.

Allie is the luscious "Boston Fern." She is the beauty of the bunch but will never admit it. She is very modest and quiet. When she does participate in worthwhile conversations, her advice and opinions are highly respected. She has many true philosophies, but she doesn't go around preaching them.

You've got to get them out of her while she's off guard. I'll bet everyone could benefit from her beliefs if she would only open up and express her thoughts. Try your hardest to get her involved in discussions. You'll be glad you did!

Curly's true identity is unknown. He was adopted while very young. It is hard to find out about the adoptee's past. The agency keeps the papers secret because it's a confidential matter. Anyway, Curly had been living everywhere, and has never been secure. His former parents (who adopted him) didn't give him the care and attention he needed. Curly's outlook on life was very negative because of his harsh upbringing. Since I've been loving him, he has almost changed his attitude completely (for the better). He still feels hate towards people who have hurt him. It will take Curly awhile to realize you want to help him, but don't give up. If you open up to him, he'll do the same to you.

Laurel and Hardy are avocado plants. Hardy is rather unusual. He grew full instead of tall and skinny like Laurel. They are just like the true comedians. If you are feeling down and depressed, they will do everything they can to cheer you up. They keep the other plants entertained with their humor and wit. It would be a gloomy place around here if it weren't for them. Although they always <u>seem</u> to be happy, it doesn't mean they really are. They need as much love as any of the others.

Piggy is the fat "Piggy-back" plant. She is really a hog, but Hoggy sounds dumb for a name. She drinks and drinks and never seems to fill up. She is still just a baby, but she is <u>huge</u> for her age. Piggy lives alongside Sonny and Cher, the fish. Every once in awhile you can catch her dipping into the fishbowl for an extra thirst-quencher. This is unusual for her breed of plant. They generally don't like to get their leaves wet. Piggy, I guess, is just unpredictable (most females are). She loves to gossip. She can tell you just about anything you need to know about other plants. When you talk to her, get ready to listen!

Nicky is my favorite one of all. I know I shouldn't play favorites, but it's hard not to. Nicky is a cousin of the well-known "Weeping Fig." He stands over five feet tall and is filled with enough love for the entire plant population. He has a personality that many of us envy. His spirit keeps everyone's hopes up, and life is never dull when you're around him. He is an all-around great guy and is well-liked by many. I'm sure you will find it a pleasure to work and care for him.

This takes care of the majority of my precious plants. The others (seeds and little sprouts) also need love and <u>lots</u> of water. That's it! Aren't they unique?

Just care for them to the best of your ability, and you'll find that they'll grow bigger and better. If you find yourself bored or depressed, just go into my room and visit "My Plant World." The plants will love your company, and best of all, they will <u>never</u> reveal any secrets that you might want to tell them. Try it sometime! It will make you feel better, and it'll make them feel loved. Thank you very much for your help!

Love,

Laurie

Laurie Zeller
Ninth Grade - 1978

For your second letter writing assignment you'll need to choose a partner. One of you writes the first letter and delivers it to your partner who reads it, answers it, and delivers the answer to you. Continue exchanging this series of letters for a week.

David,

It's very hard to write such a long letter to someone I don't even know. This letter probably won't be very interesting.

I guess I'll tell you about the Honor Society field trip I went on yesterday. It was pretty fun, but lots of people were tired on the way back.

We left at eight a.m. on the bus. It was raining all the way to Berkeley, where we went to the Lawrence Hall of Science. It has quite interesting scientific things. One huge, dark room was full of things about astrology. There were telescopes where you could see stars on a wall with rainbows that weren't really there. Another room was full of computers. There was one named Uncle Charlie that asked you questions and talked to you.

One of my friends lost her wallet, so that delayed us. I don't think she'll get it back.

We went to Golden Gate Park afterwards and ate lunch. After that the bus dropped us off at the beginning of the bridge and we walked it. The bus picked us up on the other end and took us back to school. We got back at about 4:00 p.m., and my friend's mother drove us home.

And that is all I can think of to write.

Christina Arbunic
Seventh Grade - 1981

•   •   •

Dear Christina,

How are things in the back of the class? I'm having a pretty good time over here. This is going to be an exciting month for me since I have so many big events coming up to look forward to, especially summer vacation. I'm fed up with school!

My father's being really hard on me, and I have to do a lot of extra work since my mother left for Japan last Friday. She must be in Tokyo by now. I really miss her.

This Wednesday I have to go to the Gateway Reading Council meeting at El Rancho Tropicana with Mr. Dowdle to receive an award and read some of my work. I can't see what's so outstanding about it, and I'm pretty nervous about reading it.

Worst of all, my piano recital is coming up in two weeks! My teacher says it'll be one of my best, but I'm still nervous about playing in front of all my friends and their parents.

I'm scared about my finals, too. I never know what to expect with my grades, and I know if I get one "C" I'll be butchered alive. I just hope I pick up the mail the day the fateful card arrives. It could alter my whole summer!

My father's expecting me to work my butt off during the summer, including going to a music camp at a Southern California university where they keep you chained to the keyboard 5 hours a day. I hope it won't be work all summer. There's already a chance of my riding down to Colorado with friend Kevin Brown at his grandma's ranch. He showed me a few pictures of the place, and they have some beautiful homes, plus a few hundred acres to do some riding. All I can do now is sit tight and hope for the best!

Sincerely yours,

David Jager
Seventh Grade - 1981

• • •

David,

How did you do in the Gateway Reading Council?

I like some sports. Softball is all right. I have not been doing too well this week because I bruised my palm batting.

I'm not a real science fan. I don't know too much about astronomy. I like computer science. It's interesting to be able to communicate with computers. Also, you can find out some interesting information from one.

When my family first moved into our house, the bedroom my sister and I share had wallpaper covered with rockets and space shuttles. I got tired of looking at them every morning, so we peeled it and steamed it off right away. We had to steam it off because the strange people that lived there before us had put the wallpaper on with rubber cement.

Now my room has lavender walls that are covered with posters of cats, dogs, and other animals.

We had ordered books from the Popcorn Book Club, but we don't anymore because the only things we liked were the posters and a few magazines. The other books were for little kids.

That's all for now.

Sincerely,

Christina Arbunic
Seventh Grade - 1981

• • •

Dear Christina,

Nice letter. You must have had a fun trip. I got a 3.6 G.P.A. last semester, but they still couldn't accept me in Honor Society. I can't stop kicking myself for getting two C's.

I guess that since it's hard to write interesting letters (because we hardly know each other), we should get to know each other better. So, in this letter

I'm going to talk about some of my hobbies and things I like to do.

As you read in my last letter, I spend a lot of time playing the piano. My teacher keeps me working hard and gives at least five pieces to work on each week. That means I have to practice an hour a day or more. That hardly gives me any time to play around on the keyboard, which I like doing most. I make up for it during the weekends anyway.

You could see in today's game that I can't stand sports. I'm terrible at softball, and I find it the most boring thing to do. I can find thousands of more interesting things to do than hitting a ball with a block of wood. It doesn't look like you enjoy sports either.

I'm a totally devoted space and science fiction nut, if you didn't notice. My room is wallpapered with pictures of all the Apollo moon missions, Viking landings, plus several models of the lunar modules. I'm working on one of the space shuttles right now, and there are about 50 different details to fill in. It's hard putting it together, but I'm sure it'll look great when I'm done with it.

This is about as much as I have to say about myself and what I do outside of school (not including parties, dances, etc. I never miss any!) Write back soon.

Sincerely yours,

David Jager
Seventh Grade - 1981

•   •   •

Dear David,

Referring to your letter, it sounds like you are very busy right now.

I haven't been thinking about the final tests at all. I don't think I'll do badly on them.

Mostly, I've been waiting for school to be out. For me, every day is the same - boring.

This summer I hope my family and I will be able to go to Disney World. We haven't been there in a long time, and now we finally have enough money to go. My grandma wants to go, also. But if she did, we wouldn't be able to see much because she walks very slowly. She won't dare go in a wheelchair.

My other grandma has been staying at my house for a week now. She has leukemia. She has had it for two years. It is very hard on my mom who has to stay home and take care of her. I feel really sorry for both of them.

When I was younger, I took piano lessons every Saturday. I didn't like them, and I dreaded practicing. I quit when I was eight because we moved.

Now, we have a big, nice piano in our house, and no one to play it.

Your mom and other people are lucky they can go to places like Japan. I have never been out of the United States, but I intend to go to Europe and Hawaii sometime in my future.

Oh, I almost forgot to answer your question. I do like sitting in the back. There is more to see. I used to sit in the very front where I got quite tired of looking at the same wall.

Sincerely,

Christina Arbunic
Seventh Grade - 1981

P.S. On the Gateway Reading Council and your piano recital and the finals, "Good Luck".

•   •   •

Dear Christina,

The Reading Council went great! Except to say I was one of the oldest kids out of all the presenters. It's amazing that all the kids that did their presentations weren't writers at all. Their teachers just rambled on how they made book covers, or puppets for plays, or filmstrips for songs, but no writing! There were only a few people older than I, but they didn't have time to read, and I was amazed when they came up and gave me compliments.

Zilpha Keatley Snyder was our guest author, and she gave some great tips on book writing. Oh, I almost forgot. The prizes we got were books: Books I Read When I Was Young and The Egypt Game by Zilpha, each one autographed by her. After the talk was over, most of the people left, but I stayed for dinner. After I was stuffed, Zylpha came on stage again and read several funny letters from young kids to her. One went like this:

25

Dear Zylpha,

Will you send me your autograph? I have a box in my room where I keep famous people in.

Then Mr. Dowdle came over to my house to celebrate with my father, sister, and I.

Sincerely yours,

David Jager
Seventh Grade - 1981

P.S. Just to remind you, I'm not a real science freak. Didn't want you to think I was a fanatic.

Assignment 5 - Logs

Keep a record of what happened during twenty-four consecutive hours in your life. Write every half hour or as often as you can. If you do this assignment more than once, you'll soon get a pretty good idea of how you've been spending your time.

6:30 a.m.

A new day! How I wish I could just turn over and go back to sleep, but I'm afraid I have to get up. Jogging is the first thing I do every morning, even though I feel like a wet noodle when I've finished.

7:30 a.m.

I'm now wide awake, freshened with a shower, and ready to eat breakfast. Every day I find myself debating on whether to eat breakfast or not.

8:30 a.m.

I just missed the bus! Now I have real problems being that my mother has already left for work. Well, I might as well take it easy for half an hour and watch cartoons. All I'll be missing is first period.

9:30 a.m.

Just arrived at school, and my feet are aching from walking in my platforms. I sure hope they'll let me in class without a cut. Ah well, this is a good time to get a P.E. excuse because we are doing track.

27

10:30 a.m.

Second period is almost over, and I'm so glad because my stomach has hunger pains. It's amazing how much food a person my size can consume!

11:30 a.m.

Mrs. Jones talks too much. Myself along with the other twenty-five sleeping bodies in this class have gotten nothing out of it all year long.

12:30 a.m.

Ten minutes left in this class. I can hardly wait. This class is terrible, especially when every word the teacher says sounds like a foreign language. It is! See what this class is doing to me?

1:30 p.m.

It's reading time now, and I find myself every day doing something, anything I can possibly do besides read. I hate to read!

2:30 p.m.

Wouldn't ya know! Today's a home track meet, so we don't have to dress down for P.E. After all I went through just to get out!

3:30 p.m.

School's out and boy, I'm glad! Nothing like a good old water fight as long as I don't get caught.

4:30 p.m.

Just arrived home, and the first thing I could think of was stretching out on the couch, in spite of the three books worth of homework I have to do. But, I drag out the old books anyway.

5:30 p.m.

Nearly finished with my homework, but not quite.

6:30 p.m.

Dinner at last! Nothing like fried chicken!

7:30 p.m.

Now it's my chance to sit back and watch "The Odd Couple" on T.V. Felix is so weird.

8:30 p.m.

Answering the phone in the middle of a T.V. program is one of my pet peeves. It has to be Mike!

9:30 p.m.

Mom's bickering at me to get off the phone. Well, I might as well hit the sack after a long, hard day.

9:30 p.m.

Night All!

Linda Jennings
Ninth Grade - 1978

10:30 a.m.

It's amazing how many different things can happen in half-an-hour. In that period of time Mr. Dowdle gave us four assignments. He keeps us working hard, but I enjoy most of it. I love his policies, especially. He just gave an assignment to people who were throwing plums in the library during his absence, telling them to write 500 to 1000 word descriptions of a plum. One student looked like he had swallowed a lemon whole. The punishment seemed to be getting to the "Plum Throwers" for, after all, it takes a lot of creativity to draw out 1000 words from a round, smooth, red ball, and some students aren't very well equipped for that kind of writing. So far, I have been keeping records of everything I have been doing in the past half-hour, and I'm spending my time writing a letter to Christina Arbunic.

11:00 a.m.

For the past half-hour I've been writing the letter. I'm not sure if I've been telling too much to a stranger, but it's about time that everybody in my class should get to know each other better. I told her about the big events coming up during this month.

11:30 a.m.

Ms. Peppit is continuing about Scandinavia. The information is very interesting. It seems like I was born to put pencil to paper and write, write, write. That's exactly what I've been doing, paying a small amount of attention to my lecture and dutifully scribbling notes on the side. It's pleasurable, but I'm looking forward to when she shows us the film on the country.

12:00 noon

The film proved to be very interesting. To my surprise it fit exactly what I thought about the country, a free, clean, medically and industrially efficient society where everybody stays nice, warm, and well-protected in the government's lap. But the film saw quickly through that form of government; boredom prevails. Drinking and alcoholism are very frequent. Juvenile delinquents, crime and violence are rather frequent. The picture looks tempting, but I'm glad I'm right here in the U.S.A.

I'm in the middle of an empty lunch conversation that has to be kept going by small pushes of vulgarity and some disgusting jokes. They're fine when you hear them, but after you think about them seriously, you find your stomach out of line. It seems that all these people (including me sometimes) are all sex, sports, and music oriented. It seems that all conversations and jokes point toward those three things. "Wanna go listen to some music? Did you hear the one about the 15 cent screw? Did you see that hit John made last night playing the Cardinals? Man! That thing went sailing!" are the things I usually hear. Nevertheless, it's just plain comforting to stay around in a group and listen to each other, even though it may be as indecent as anything!

12:30 p.m.

I've been spending my time reading an article on U.F.O.'s in <u>Read Magazine</u>. It's pretty fun and amusing.

1:00 p.m.

Ms. Branvold is showing us how to do book mapping. The method is pretty boring, but it seems fun to draw out and complete.

1:30 p.m.

It's about time to leave for math, and I'm anticipating my test grades. I expect to get at least a "C" or "B" on one of them. For the rest of the time I'm talking to my friends.

2:00 p.m.

I've been in math for about half an hour. I'm absolutely shocked! I've got an "F" for my area and circumference test, and a "C-" on my make-up for area and perimeter. For the rest of the time I'm listening to the lecture.

2:30 p.m.

The lecture is finished and we have to complete a sheet on finding the area of rectangular solids. When I think of it, I really am interested in geometry and mathematics, but all that has been marred with my past experience with math.

3:00 p.m.

I've been waiting for the bus to come and watching all the activity going on between students. They seem to be happy just sitting around and talking to each other.

3:30 p.m.

I'm eating my snack at a table right now. I spent most of my time looking out the window on the bus while the others screamed and yelled in the back. I knew I didn't want to join them, but if I didn't laugh or look at some of the things they did, I'd find myself square and repressive.

4:00 p.m.

I'm having a fascinating time reading "Flowers for Algernon," the story of a retarded man experiencing extreme intellectual growth and suddenly finding himself on the other side of the intellectual fence. It also explores the conflict between his old self and his new super intellectual self.

4:30 p.m.

I've been working on my math, and then taped a funny interview with my sister. She played a super eccentric pianist while I was a conventional interviewer. It was hilarious, and we couldn't stop laughing when she went into her hysterical fits.

5:00 p.m.

I've started my piano practice after spending half an hour working on this assignment. It's really interesting to work on when you think about it.

6:00 p.m.

I was very concentrated during my practice today, so I decided to make an account of the last hour instead of half an hour. What a miracle it is to let yourself get absorbed in a concentrated hour of work! Everything surrounding you seems to fade, leaving only you and the music. Time flies during such moments. What I find most surprising is the way an hour passes in what you thought was fifteen minutes. I also think it's amazing that the number of objects around you is suddenly forgotten. When I came to the end of a practice, I suddenly became aware again of my surroundings. "There's the window! And there is the couch!" I find myself saying when I look around and become familiar once again with the daily world.

6:30 p m.

We had a fascinating conversation about art and photography. My sister's argument was that even though photography showed you exactly what was there, painting was more accurate because it gave you the feel and sensual imagery of the place. We found that in both painting and writing you could smell, see, even feel the place the artist or author was portraying.

7:00 p.m.

I've been helping Sheila do the dishes and clean. Since Mother has been gone, Pa expects a lot more of us in terms of work. We are always arguing about something, but most of all, we get along.

7:30 p.m.

I've started reading the <u>Two Towers</u> by Tolkien after breathlessly finishing <u>The Fellowship of the Ring</u>. There is something magical about Tolkien's writing that won't let you put the book down. The air seems to change when you read his descriptions. When he describes the dark forests of Mirkwood, everything turns gray, and when he describes the bright lands of Lothlorien, the entire world grows golden, sweet, and singing. You always feel like one of the group when you read a Tolkien adventure.

8:00 p.m.

I'm still absorbed in my reading. At this point, Frodo and companions, including Gandalf the Wizard, are traveling through the halls of Moria.

9:00 p.m.

The reading was too engrossing to interrupt. Frodo has left the halls of Moria after a battle with an army of Orcs. While crossing a narrow stone bridge to escape from them, a balrog comes from the water and seizes Gandalf, dragging him to his fate.

6:30 a.m.

Good morning! I had a good sleep, even though I felt like a log when I got up. I'm late for breakfast as usual, and I have to start my morning mad rush to get ready before Tenna comes to pick me up.

7:00 a.m.

Tenna came, and we're waiting at the bus stop. I usually have enough time to make finishing touches on my homework while I wait for the bus.

7:30 a.m.

The bus has come, and I'm on my way to school. I usually keep quiet on the way.

8:00 a.m.

I'm in class right now after finishing some school business. Now it's time for the Pledge of Allegiance and the morning bulletin.

8:30 a.m.

Paul Huberty and I have just completed a small telephone exercise assignment. It's amusing to perform on stage in front of the class, and I find it more enjoyable every time I do it.

9:00 a.m.

Right now I have come to gym. We watched the other exercises 'til the end of the period in Drama. A lot of them were hilarious.

10:00 a.m.

I decided not to bring my notebook outside, being involved in a fast-moving game of speed-a-way. It's great fun to run around the field. It gives one a sense of control. I'm still having problems with other students, especially during roll call. A lot of the students can't miss a chance of giving me a good punch before the P.E. teacher arrives to take roll. A lot of it has gone too far, so far that the teacher gave me her personal permission to rearrange the face of my chief tormentor. I can't wait 'til Monday when I can improve his looks!

10:30 a.m.

Here I am again, back from where I started. I spent the break discussing a new band we're forming. I think that with enough musical people in our group, the whole project could turn out to be an exciting and enjoyable experience. For the last half hour I've been working on other assignments, and now I've completed this one. That's all for a "Day in the Life of David Jager."

David Jager
Seventh Grade - 1981

Assignment 6 – Diaries

Write a paper titled "A Day in the Life of _____ ." You may wish to use the information from the previous assignment, your log, and write up that specific day, or you may wish to speak more generally and write up a composite day, one which sums up how your days usually go. A write up of either a particular day in your life or a general impression of how a day in your life passes is acceptable. Try both if you have time.

"A Day in the Life of Kelly Boyce"

Today I got up sore and hurting bad from a terrible sunburn. I got up at six o'clock and took a shower. Then I dried and curled my hair, got dressed (very carefully) and ate breakfast, a whole bowl of Cheerios. I left for school at 7:30 a.m. At 8:00 first period began. I am in English writing this assignment.

9:00 a.m. I'm in second period class, math with Ms. Branvold. I took a quiz. It wasn't very hard. I hope I did good on it.

At 9:50 a.m. it was snack break. I couldn't find my friend and looked all over for her. I finally found her, and she said she had to clean desks in math class.

At 10:10 a.m. break was over and third period began. It was history, and we have groups called "wagon trains". It's pretty neat, but you have to do a lot of extra credit!

Now 11:05 a.m. begins art class. I finished a painting of a lake, mountains, and high-flying clouds. It was in different shades of blue.

11:55 a.m. starts lunch break. I met my friends at my locker, and then we went to the cafeteria to get our lunch. We sat out on the side of the school that faces Middle Rincon Road. Some kids started a food fight, so we left. Lunch ended at 12:30 p.m., and we went to our fifth period class. At this time, the whole school has to read for twenty minutes. After reading period I had P.E. We played softball, and it killed my sunburn. Ouch! But our team won anyway.

Sixth period started at 1:45 p.m. in science class. This class is a drag for me. I find it uninteresting and boring (yawn!). But the best thing of all is it's the last class of the day!

After school my mom, her friend, my little sister, and I went down to the auto shop to pick up my mom's friend's car. After that we went home and relaxed. I rode down to the store with my brother. Then I rode my bike up to my friend's house. I had to ride up a hill, and it was hard. I collapsed as soon as I got in her house. She was glad I "dropped in". She's my best friend.

I went home at 5:00 and set the dinner table. We ate dinner, and after dinner I went to my room to study. It was finally my brother's week to do dishes, so I didn't have to bother with that.

Later, my mom, my little sister, and I went to our friend's house. Candy is my mom's friend, and Carolyn, her daughter, is my friend. Carolyn and I went into her room, listened to music, and gossiped. We watched some boys outside play baseball, but we got tired of that.

We got home at about 9:30 p.m., and then I crashed into bed because I was so tired.

And that is part of one of my boring 24 hour days.

Kelly Boyce
Eighth Grade - 1981

"A Day in the Life of David Jager"

There was a mad rush that particular morning. I was late, Tenna was early, my things weren't organized, and breakfast was cold. We shoved off in the cold morning air to the bus stop. The bus was late, like usual, and was an old junky model a garbage lot would refuse. It inched us to the school and let us off. I waited for the halls to open, and when they finally did, it was Paul's turn to use his locker first. I waited around and used mine, after it was kicked shut by Cheryl McCarter four times. I grabbed my things and fumbled into the Drama room. People were sweet and sarcastic like usual, and one student was putting on his freaky acts. No matter how noisy his are, they can't stand the sound of my playing the piano, even though they like to bang on it themselves.

I ambled on to P.E. to assume my role of punching bag. Brett Wittmer would do anything to make me fight him. I was kicked around until Ms. King-Claye came and took roll, and we went out to the field to play speed-a-way. I had a fun time even though we lost. I came into English after a fight about the band during break, and for once I was a little bit in control.

World Geography was next, followed by lunch. Then I rushed off to reading and listened to Ms. Branvold while I was anticipating my grades in math. I came to math and sat quietly in my desk and waited. I was appalled when I saw that I had a "D" and "C-". I gathered up my stuff at the bell and went to the bus stop. I couldn't risk getting my fingers jammed by Cheryl after school anymore.

Home was a relief. I spent my time practicing and reading by myself, and enjoyed a large dinner. School and all my other troubles were forgotten in another world. Oh, I almost forgot to tell. It was a pretty good day for me at school.

David Jager
Seventh Grade - 1981

Assignment 7 - Autobiographical Sketches

Think of an event in the past which has influenced your life more than any other event. Write about that event and how it has made your life different from what it used to be.

For your second assignment, make up a "fictional" person and write about an important happening in that person's life.

"Junior High School"

Although it's been quite a while ago, I still remember my first day in junior high school. I got up early that morning and dressed in what I had planned the night before. I ate heartily and got to the bus stop fifteen minutes early. When I entered the bus, I was shocked to find that no one would let me sit down. I guess they wanted a seat to themselves. It seemed like forever, but finally I reached the back of the bus, and someone sacrificed just enough room for me to sit. I could tell already that the day was going to turn out to be a disaster.

After getting off the bus, I followed the crowd and ended up sitting on bleachers in the back of the gym. After a short speech from the principal, we were sent to different classes where we would be given further instruction. I was given a locker number and a slip which told me the other five classes I would attend that day.

After that, the whirling started. Rules, due dates, and requirements were thrust upon me. I was awakened from the daze by a bell. Everyone jumped up, so I did, too. Second and third periods were just as bad. At last it was lunchtime! I walked to the snack bar, thinking of how privileged I was to now be able to choose whatever I wanted to eat. This was not allowed in elementary school. I arrived only to find a bunch of animals wildly pushing to get to the front of the line. In my state of amazement, I got at the end of the line. The food was bad, but no worse than it had been at my last school. I dreaded the moment when the bell rang, and it was time to go to fourth period.

I was instructed to get a pencil before, so I went to my locker where I had put them. Upon finding that I had lost the combination, I panicked. What would they do to me? I was doomed! After convincing myself that there would be no severe punishment, I found the office and got a new copy of my combination. I went through fourth and fifth periods totally distressed.

Come sixth period, my paper said that I was to go to the gym. I didn't know where it was, and feeling rather stupid, I asked an older-looking girl. I suffered through P.E. and fortunately got on the bus and was delivered home. I repeated this entire story to each member of my family and swore that I would never forget that day.

Jill Joyce
Eighth Grade - 1972

"Birth Order"

I think the most important event in my life was being born the last child.

I think that if I had been the first child in my family, I would have had many more responsibilities dumped in my lap. I think a lot more things would have been expected of me. Also, I would have had two bratty younger brothers.

If I had been the middle child, I would have responsibilities, but not as many as my older brother. I would look up to him and try to be "Big" and do what he did. I would look down upon my younger brother, sometimes, and be bossy other times. I would help him and show him how to do things.

I am sometimes glad that I am the youngest, and sometimes not. Things are expected of me, but not as much as my two older brothers. The times when I wish I were the oldest are when both my brothers are bossing me around. I wish that I could boss them around and yell at them with out them hitting me back!

Sometimes, I wish I were the middle child so I could be friends and talk to an older brother, and yet still be looked up to by a younger brother.

But I happen to be stuck with being the third and last child, and there's nothing I can do about it!

Suzanne Dieter
Seventh Grade - 1981

"The New Corpus Eaton 412"

The year is 3008, and finally man has found a way to immortality! It was simple: no drugs, no miracle pills, no chemical aids of any kind. It works out like a car. When the engine runs down, a person buys a new one and is fine. Now, humans can live as long as they want by buying new bodies.

My name is Eaton 412, and I am a prime corpus, fresh from the factory. I am complete with precision-working brain and nervous system, and all of my organs have received The Good Housekeeping Seal of Approval. My skin is guaranteed to last and retain color for a lifetime or your money back. My facial details are also sculpted in the latest fashionable looks for men. Blood surrogates are made 100% germ resistant with cell nutrients included for good health. Sex hormone levels are high, and reproductive system organs are working at the peak of efficiency. Spermatozoa (if desired) are fashioned to give your children your desired genetic traits, including emotional characteristics. The digestive system is complete, and the stomach is double lined to prevent ulcers. The intestines are compactly designed to absorb ten times more food nutrients per square inch than normal human capacity. The skeletal system is designed to resist pressures up to 100 pounds per square inch and is made of an ultra-pure, silicate-organic mixture for an extremely light and fracture-resistant skeletal structure.

Muscles are made to perform super athletic feats and resist stress, preventing arthritic conditions. My brain is designed and compacted to retain more information, and knowledge of complete fields can be programmed into me by the computers at the buyer's request. The buyer's entire knowledge -emotional, factual, and autonomic- will be emptied from him and can be programmed into the likes of me by computer.

I can be obtained with a down payment of only $13,000 with 20% interest added to the balance paid in monthly installments. Find me at fine body-shops everywhere!

David Jager
Seventh Grade- 1981

"Self Encounter"

Hello, my name is Margaret Learie, and I am a fifth grade student at Montessouri Central School. I have a pretty fun time here even though things get difficult sometimes. Everything seems to be fairly normal at my school. When something really crazy happens, like someone looking just like you (appearing all of a sudden), you just don't believe it, and go on doing your homework or eating your sandwich. I never believed it!

It was a hot Monday morning when I was walking to my school. The air was ablaze, and it scorched my skin. I walked towards the playground, just being myself, feeling awful hot and fanning myself with a book. It was 8:00 o'clock when it happened. I didn't know <u>how</u> it happened, it just did! It was an event that jumped out at me like a monster in a spook ride at the fair, and it shook me to bits!

I saw another me, walking!

She was there walking by herself, plain as day. She had my own eyes, my nose, my lips. She even <u>acted</u> like me! I gasped and ran to the classroom.

Mrs. Nesbitt was sitting at her desk, calm as you please, correcting test papers from last Friday. She is my English teacher, and I am one of her best students. I rushed into her room.

"Mrs. Nesbitt! Come quick!" I said breathlessly.

"What's the matter?" she said coolly. "You seem to be in a hurry this morning." She smiled, and I quickly smiled back.

"Look, Mrs. Nesbitt, you gotta come right now! There's this girl, and she looks all like me, and I don't know who she is, and . . .!"

"Calm down," said Mrs. Nesbitt, folding her hands, looking sort of puzzled at me.

"But you got to come see it now!" I cried. I looked towards the window. The girl was standing there, smiling. I jumped up and pointed towards her. "Look!" I yelled. She vanished from sight. Mrs. Nesbitt leaned over her desk and looked towards the window.

"I don't see anything . . ."

"But she was there a minute ago, standing right there and smiling. . .!"

"I suggest you go to the nurse's office," she said. There was a worried look on her face. It was hopeless. I ran out of the room, crying. I didn't know what to do. Maybe I <u>should</u> go to the nurse. Maybe I was going <u>crazy</u> or something!

Five minutes later I was lying on a cot with a cold towel on my head. The nurse said it was just the heat and nothing about which to worry. But I kept thinking about that girl. I couldn't get my mind off her.

That afternoon Mrs. Nesbitt gave me permission to go to the library. She gives me lots of special privileges, and some people get jealous of me. Ours is a pretty large library and has lots of books on science and stuff. I picked out a large book from the shelf and brought it to the reading table. It was really weird. It talked about some things called clones and how they could make one person from another and make them look exactly alike. I checked it out and read further. It was then when things started to fall into place. I never learned so much in my life! It talked about D.N.A. and ribosomes and mitochondria, and it said that every cell in a person's body had the information to make that person again, and that's how clones were made.

Could that girl be my clone? I don't remember giving cell samples or whatever they call them. Could I have been cloned when I was born? I walked home after school, thinking about it.

I walked through the front door and sat down at the table, feeling dizzy. Mom came into the kitchen.

"Hi!"

"Hi, Maggie. Boy, you sure look tired!"

"Got a snack?"

"Sure, cookies and milk in a minute." She came back with a tray of assorted cookies and a tall glass of milk.

"Mom?"

"Mm?"

"Did I ever give any blood samples?"

"Yes, when you were born," she said. "Why do you ask?"

I looked out towards the old wooden porch and the small asphalt road that lay beyond. The dry wind swept the dusty landscape and warmed the drowsy air. I sat back in my chair.

"Just wondering," I said. "Just wondering."

David Jager
Seventh Grade 1981

Assignment 8 - Memoirs

Write about a person, pet, or place you once knew very well, but because of death, moving, or other circumstances, you are no longer together or close. Try to give your audience a clear idea of what the person, pet, or place described was like when you knew her, him, or it.

"Connie"

Students and faculty of Rincon Valley Junior High School were grief stricken Wednesday by the news of the untimely death of Connie Elizabeth So, outstanding seventh grade student.

Connie was born on May 23, 1966 at Stanford Hospital in Palo Alto, California. She lived in Santa Rosa for the past three years. Before coming to Rincon Valley Junior High School last September, Connie attended Binkley Elementary School.

Mr. Moberly, principal of Binkley, remembers Connie as being a super girl, bright, always happy, and as he put it, "A girl with a little bit of sunshine." While at Binkley, Connie was active in the play, "Oliver."

Mr. Austin, sixth grade teacher at Binkley, recalls, "Connie was a beautiful person and a dear friend. I will always remember her delightful sense of humor and smiling face. She contributed so much in enriching the lives of all who were fortunate enough to know her. It is very difficult for me to realize she is no longer with us. I will miss her very much."

Before coming to Rincon, Connie was active in Brownies and 4 H. She loved reading and horses. During the few short months that she was with us at Rincon, she was active in gymnastics, Honor Society, and Camera Club. Her openness, smile, personality, and friendliness will long be remembered by her many friends.

Mr. Milkoff, seventh grade World Geography teacher, summarized the feelings of most of us when he said, "Connie So was the epitome of a beautiful human being. She was warm, sensitive, happy, and caring. She brought a refreshing breath of life into our hearts. I will always remember her smile and her sincerity. We have not lost Connie for she will always be with us."

"Connie's void can only be filled with a sincere desire to emulate her life style. Her cheerfulness, helpfulness, friendliness, and all around thoughtfulness will always be a goal for which to strive," added Mr. Beal, seventh grade math teacher.

We will all miss Connie. The following message from Mrs. Riddel, sixth grade teacher at Binkley, sums up the feelings of all of us:

"Just as a lovely star passes through the heavens, so Connie passed through our lives - brilliant and brightening all she touched. The essences of her beauty,
intelligence, wit and laughter will be with us
to remember for years
to remember with tears
to remember with joy
to remember Connie."

John Hogan
Eighth Grade - 1979

"Nona"

My grandma died when I was four. She died of a heart attack. I remember my mom trying to explain to me that Grandma wasn't going to visit any more. She said that she was up in heaven, and that she was happy and okay. It was very hard for me to accept that fact because I loved my Nona (Nona means "Grandma" in Italian) very much!

That night I remember having a very scary dream. I dreamed that all my relatives and family were sitting in chairs around my living room when suddenly Nona grasped her heart, yelled out a horrible moan, and fell on the floor. The strange thing about it was that everyone there didn't even notice! When I saw this,

I ran beside her and yelled and yelled for someone to help her. And that's when I woke up. I woke up caked in sweat, my heart beating fast, and with tears streaming down my face. It was one of the most scary experiences I have ever had.

I got out of bed and ran to my mom. I didn't tell her about the dream but just cried in her lap. She tried to ask me what was wrong, but I was crying so hard I couldn't speak. I didn't tell her about it until I was five. Then all of a sudden it came bursting out of me! It was like an explosion. The day was nothing special, just a normal day. I told her the dream, every last detail of it. She explained to me that Nona had died in a chair in her own home. Finally, I did accept the fact that my Nona was gone and let my worries drift away.

In the years to come, I would think about her. Usually at night, when I was in bed, I would go over in my mind the memories of her. And then sometimes I would cry. Soft cries, so nobody would hear. For I was embarrassed at being as old as nine and still be thinking about her and sometimes crying about her.

Suzanne Dieter
Seventh Grade - 1981

"Grandpa"

Last December about one week before Christmas something happened that made a big change in my life. One of my closest relatives died. It was my grandpa. His death struck me hard and made me feel like there was a big empty space in me.

He had been ill for a long time, had had eye operations, and had cancer throughout his body. He had to have his voice box removed because of cancer, and it left a hole in his throat. He coughed constantly and had to learn to talk all over again. I tried to help him as much as I could, and I know it was hard for him, but he tried. It was hard for people to understand him because they would get nervous and tense up around him. He would have to repeat what he was trying to say over and over again, and he would get so frustrated that he would nearly cry.

About two weeks before Christmas I heard from my grandma, and she said that my grandpa had gotten really sick and hardly moved or talked at all. He wouldn't eat or drink anything, and he started to dehydrate. I begged my parents to let me go and try to help my grandpa, but they said it was no use because my grandpa had suffered so much that he had just given up on living.

One week before Christmas my dad called me and told me that my grandpa was dead. I felt sorry for myself for awhile, locked myself up in my room, and hardly spoke or ate.

I thought my life was over. Then one day I thought everything through and realized that it was stupid for me to feel sorry for myself. I had to go on living just like everyone else. My family comforted me during that time, and I comforted them in return. We made it through because we knew we had to.

Kelly Boyce
Eighth Grade - 1981

"Heidi Lee of Heidelberg"

I remember her very well. She was short, fat, and lovable. She was intelligent, too. I didn't feed her very much because whenever she was hungry, she would yelp on someone's doorstep. Everyone in the neighborhood loved her, and she loved them. Her affection was overwhelming, and she showed it by putting her cold nose on your feet.

In a way she was an unusual dog. Unlike any other I knew, she enjoyed swimming. It got very hot where we used to live, and upon an invitation from Heidi, we both dove into the pool. Actually, she just slid in feet first.

She was a constant friend to me when no one else was there to play with. I had her for ten years, and never did she let me down. Being a child, I loved her more each day. The shock of her death was something I'll never forget. I wanted to die right along with her. For a long time I didn't even want to see another dog, but now I have one. It doesn't make me sad to think about her anymore. I like to remember the wonderful times we had. Even though I love the dog I have now, she is still not as lovable as Heidi.

Jill Joyce
Eighth Grade - 1972

"Stormy"

It was a stormy, misty night, and I was only five years old when my father brought me home a present. It was a beautiful, white, Arabian horse! He was

47

covered with dirt and very nervous like myself because the last time I rode a horse, I fell off and broke my nose!

I decided to name the horse "Stormy." He was fifteen years old and had been crippled from eating too much and exercising too little. My dad said we'd work him back into shape, and so we did. I rode him for at least an hour a day, no matter if it was storming or a hundred degrees heat outside. On weekends I rode him all day and then gave him a bath.

Stormy grew to be twenty-five years old and unruly! He would buck when a person tried to ride him.

Once, late on a cold December night, I went to feed him, but he was lying on his side, giving off a sorrowful groan. I ran to him, called his name, and tried to get him to stand, but he wouldn't move! I screamed to my mom as I fell beside Stormy, trying to see if he was still alive, for the groaning had stopped! His eyes glanced at me. I was relieved to see that he was still alive, but scared of the thought that he might be dying! My mom dropped me off at a friend's house because she didn't want me to have to see Stormy die.

The next day when I got home, Stormy was still there and alive. My mom explained that he was suffering and would have to be put away. I couldn't stand the thought of it because I knew that when a horse died, he was sent to the glue factory. Tears crept down my cheeks as my horse, my friend, was being carried away!

Linda Jennings
Ninth Grade - 1978

"Cookie"

When I was little, my mom got me a kitten. We named her "Cookie" because she loved cookies. I used to tie a string to her flea collar and drag her around like a dog. I liked to dress her up in doll clothes and wrap her up in baby blankets and sing her lullabies. At night when I had to go to bed, I would sneak Cookie into bed with me and hide her under my covers when my dad came down the hall. She would stick her cold, wet nose in my ear and purr me to sleep.

One day I spent the night at my friend's house. It was foggy that night. In the morning I went home and opened the door to see my mom with a tear-washed face. She said, "There's something I have to tell you, Kelly, and I want you to listen." I had no idea what the problem was, and I was nervous. "Cookie got hit by a car last night." I didn't know what to say, so I started to cry. My cat was my best friend, and now she was gone. I was sad!

I have had only one cat since then, and it was a lazy one. It would run away for awhile and come back when it was hungry, but it could never compare with Cookie.

Kelly Boyce
Eighth Grade - 1981

"Cooke City"

During the summer vacations I spent in Cooke City, I loved to sit in my aunt and uncle's old-fashioned general store and read comic books. I would sit on an ancient, wooden bench, eat chocolate I had picked from the front counter on the way by, and read comics. I thought it was heaven to be safe from the rain or heat and just read comics.

There must have been over twenty of them sitting on the ugly, black rack which seemed out of place in the middle of all the wood cabinets and shelves, but I loved them. I might spend three hours a day in there just reading through them.

They never got old, even though I knew many by heart. The metal rack and collection of somewhat dirtied comic books were always there waiting, and those same comics are now packed away in a trunk of memories, just waiting for me to unpack and remember.

Jennifer Higham
Seventh Grade - 1979

"The Ideal Holiday"

It was early in the morning when we left for Assisi in Italy. We had worked the entire week, and now we set out at 5:00 a.m. to visit the fabled Italian town where St. Francis was born. We packed our bags with sandwiches and guide books and set out for the train station. When we arrived, the train was just pulling in, brakes screeching it to a halt, smoke and vapors surrounding it.

During the ride I spent my time looking through the window, watching the landscape slowly brighten with the first rays of the famous, well-loved Italian sun. A city emerged from the distant mountains -- Assisi. It lay there, shining brightly among the large, verdant hills. We arrived fifteen minutes later at a modest train station, very neat and well-kept, lined with potted geraniums.

What followed was a long walk through the Italian countryside. The air was cold and fresh, the landscape new, shining golden in the sunlight. We walked up the mountains to our destination, a bright patch of white light against the green hills. It lay in the forest surrounded by tall stone walls, built centuries ago.

We walked through the painted basilicas and ancient squares and visited the monasteries and convents lost in the mists of time. We strolled through ancient vistas and narrow alleys, the remainders of a lost and forgotten time. The sun was dipping down towards the horizon, glowing a deep red. We walked back to the station and took the last train home.

David Jager
Seventh Grade - 1981

Assignment 9 - Biographical Sketches

Interview a person until you discover information about an <u>important part</u> of his/her life. When you do, write it up. One approach is to get the person talking about his/her childhood experiences. As the interview continues, try to discover what events in the person's life helped him/her to become the person he/she is today. Talking to older people and younger people than yourselves will make this assignment interesting and challenging for you, but you may work with a classmate if you wish.

"David Wilson"

David Wilson is a very superstitious, understanding, and mellow person. He is aware of himself and others. At times he feels insecure. What makes David superstitious are things like dreams coming true or playing a basketball game with his socks rolled down and winning the game and thinking the reason he won was because his socks were rolled down.

David never puts on a mask in front of people, and everyone really likes him for who he is. He doesn't care to be around the same people all the time, but he is just friendly with everyone and accepts people for whom they are.

David is a member of a big family. He sometimes has a communication gap with his parents. He was born in Berkeley on June 9, 1960. When he was six, David's family moved to a ranch in Cloverdale. David claims that Cloverdale was the place he really was raised. During his stay there, he said he did a lot of fun but dumb things. In fifth grade he was upset because he was going to leave his home and come to Santa Rosa. Leaving his friends wasn't going to be easy. At the present time, David has lived in Santa Rosa for three and one-half years and likes it.

David enjoys many different activities. Skiing is one of his favorites. "Getting out in the fresh air feels great!" he said. The radio in David's room is turned on as soon as he wakes up, and it stays on about three hours every day. He usually goes to sleep by the radio, too. David really absorbs himself in music. Fishing is another activity he enjoys. Sometimes he's not too successful, but, he says, "It's the fun that counts!"

Before David moved to Cloverdale, his family stayed in a cabin in the mountains. This was for one summer. He used to go fishing every day at a little, peaceful pond. One day he went fishing with his whole family. His dad was attempting to catch a fish, but he had to leave it to go help his wife worm a hook. He handed the pole to David who felt a tremendous tug and screamed! Gradually, David slowly reeled in his first catch. He walked all around, showing everyone his great sixteen inch fish.

That night at dinner David said he wanted to eat his catch all by himself. His parents said it was O.K. He sat down at the dinner table and attempted to eat this fish that was spread across his whole plate. He plunged his fork into the fish and started taking bite after bite after bite. Soon, he was getting tired and full, and after only half the fish was gone, he left the table. I doubt if he'll ever try that again.

David enjoys listening to the radio, and he enjoys the life he leads. He likes Rincon Valley Junior High School and all the people there he knows. In the future he would like to be a writer, sketch artist, and/or a musician. I'm sure that whatever he decides to be, he will be good at because of his understanding of life, people, and himself.

Cindy Stipes
Eighth Grade - 1974

"Ana Frey"

Anna Frey has done much for herself and her community during the last eighty years of her life. She has lived to tell of World Wars I and II, the Great Depression, and many other major events in world history that affected her life.

Anna was born in Vienna, Austria in 1907. Her family was very well-to-do, and she lived a happy and comfortable childhood. Unlike the average child today, Anna was nursed and taken care of by her nanny and governess for many years in her early life. She was always very close with her family and relatives, which was common with families such as hers. One person that was very influential in Anna's childhood was her aunt, with whom she often traveled.

Anna attended a private girls' school in the suburbs of Vienna for most of her high school years. Afterwards, she attended a business school and then a millinery school to learn a trade at which she could make money if she had to. However, ladies such as Anna were never usually expected to work, but instead were supposed to get married and have children. Education was always important to Anna, and it later came in handy when she had to support her husband and herself as newcomers to America with little money. In school, one of Anna's best friends was her cousin, so she didn't spend much time socializing with other girls. Anna always liked school, and she was especially good at math, but in some ways it was hard for her because she had a minor case of dyslexia.

Dating in Anna's teenage years was a serious matter that was never usually pursued until a girl reached sixteen or seventeen. Anna really worries about teenagers today because there are so many temptations such as sex, drugs, alcohol, etc. In her day, teenagers were happier and not so pressured, although parents were strict about what their children did and where they went.

Anna Frey's life was greatly affected throughout World War I and the Great Depression. She was always aware of some outside, ongoing world event, partly because her family suffered financially at times. Many people went hungry then, but her family tried its best to help those who were not as fortunate as they.

In 1938, when Hitler became a threat to Austria, many thought the whole affair would blow over, but Anna and Hans, her husband of four years, knew trouble was coming and fled to England and then on to America where they would spend the rest of their lives. To this day, Anna can still remember hearing the sound of the Nazis marching on the streets of Vienna. Her brother had also fled, to Australia, and her sister to India, but her parents were not so fortunate. They were taken to a concentration camp where they barely survived on potato peelings for two years. They never really recovered from their lack of nutrition, and they never wanted to talk about their experience in the camp after they finally reached America.

When Anna was thirty-one and Hans, a doctor of law, was forty-two, they reached America with less than ten dollars between them and no work. It was during the Great Depression, and the unemployment rate was extremely high, but Anna kept her spirits up and began making hats to support her husband and herself until he found a job. Anna knew that the one thing no one could ever take from her was her education. They lived in Chicago and remained there for the next forty-five years.

Anna became interested in social work because of her love for people, and she began to get involved in the community. Her job as a social worker included involvement in the Housing committee, neighborhood watch, and other community groups.

When Anna became seventy-seven years old and her husband was eighty-eight, they agreed that moving to a warmer, sheltered environment where they could be helped out would be better for them. So, that year, 1984, they moved to the Friends' House Retirement Home in Santa Rosa, California.

So far, they have been at the Friends' House for three years and they love it! They have a lot of neighbors and friends with whom they talk and go places, and Anna is still involved in community work which she enjoys very much.

Anna is a very courageous woman. She came to America with nothing but hope and faith that she would find a better and happier life for Hans and herself. And she did. Anna has spent forty-five years of her life helping others make better lives for themselves just because she liked people and cared.

Indeed, Anna Frey is a very special woman!

Sheba Fulton
Ninth Grade - 1987

Assignment 10 - Biographical Sequences -

Plays Developing Generalizations

Select a biography or autobiography from the library. As you read it, make <u>single sentence statements</u> which tell the most important things that can be said about the person's life. When you're finished with the book, study the <u>single sentence statements</u> you've made and try to identify the key quality or dominant factor in the person's life and state it as a <u>single sentence generalization</u>. Now write a <u>short play</u> which develops this <u>generalization</u> and in which the person read about becomes the main character. Include some interior and dramatic monologue in the play.

With other students, memorize the lines and produce the play for the class. You, the writer, should take the part of the main character.

"Jim Ryan"

Generalization: Jim Ryan was determined to win the race and break the world's record in the classic mile.

Act I.

Scene I: All-American Invitational Track Meet, July 17, University of California's Edwards Field. It is time for the classic mile run. Jim is all set for the race and has built up confidence throughout the day. The runners now line up for the start.

Starter: Runners -- to your mark! Get set! (The gun explodes with a crack; the runners are off.)

55

Jim: (To himself) Keep cool. Stay relaxed. Even if Von Ruden and Romo are out ahead first off, I must save as much energy as possible.

Timer: (Shouting the 220 yard mark times) 220, 29.3! (As Jim runs by)

Jim: Oh, oh. 29.3. I'd better watch it, or it will be another "Compton." Our pace is lagging a bit, also. We might not make the record. What's this? Romo passing von Ruden on the first lap? He is really picking up; I'll have to follow his pace to win.

Timer: (Shouting the first lap times) First lap, 57.7! (As Jim runs by)

Jim: 57.7! Boy, I felt sure I did something over 59. Just stay with Romo. Stay close so you're not knocked out later. Now Von Ruden is lagging. Take him. Take him now! Bell is coming up behind. Take him, boy! (Jim passes Von Ruden with Bell on his heels.) Romo has really quickened the pace now. I can feel the change noticeably.

Timer: (Shouting 600 times) 600 yards, 1:25.8! (Jim glides past.)

Jim: My legs are getting heavy. Just like at "Compton." I may be getting tired. Loosen up, now. Keep cool. My bad knee is burning, though. (Jim swerves his eyes for a glance to his outside.) Oh, oh! Bell is passing me. He is even passing Romo. I must keep up with him! He can't win! Here comes two laps, already!

Timer: (Again shouting second lap time) Two laps. 1:55.5!

Jim: My legs don't feel heavy anymore! I feel great! You're going good, Jim. That first half was fast! Just keep up with Bell! Stay with him until he slows! I've got to! (Jim puts more into it.) He's slowing now! I have to pass him. I must get the record. After this curve, take him! Now!

(Jim shoots past Bell and takes the lead.)

Good! I feel great! You're really going nice, Jim. Boy, I even feel more mentally awake! (Jim looks over each shoulder.) They are really falling back, now. Am I going too fast? Maybe I won't even finish at this fast pace. Just keep cool. This is my race now. Keep relaxed! But, can I go faster?

(The next few moments are filled with people shouting eagerly.)

Go, Jim! Now, go! (He thrusts forward at greater speed.)

Timer: (Shouting the two and one-half lap time) Two and one-half laps, 2:25.6!

Jim: Careful now! Not too fast or you won't make it! Still one and a half laps to go!

(The crowd screams wildly now.)

Timer: (Shouting the 3 lap time) Three laps, 2:55.3!

Jim: Can I do it in . . . maybe 3.50? You must make this last lap in 58 seconds! You're tired, Jim, but press, PRESS! Now, only 300 yards to go! Turn on your drive! Come on! (Jim tries but cannot.) Sprint! Sprint, Jim! Go! Don't tie up! Sprint!

Timer: (Shouting the three and one-half lap time) Three and one-half laps, 3:23.3!

Jim: 200 yards to go! Explode! Pull your Peter Snell and explode! -- I can't! (Jim could not "explode," and he realized it.) At least maintain your speed, Jim. If nothing else, keep your speed. Come on, Jim, go! Even if it hurts! The name of the game is pain! Drop your arms and drive, Jim!

(Jim whirls past the finish line.)

Jim: Now, I can only hope and wait for the record.

Announcer: (Over loud speaker) Winning time in the mile, 3:51.3, a new world record set by Jim Ryan!

(Crowd roars and cheers loudly.)

Jim: (throwing up his arms) I did it!

(Crowd gathers around Jim to congratulate him.)

Daryl Nelson
Seventh Grade - 1969

Assignment 11 - Biographical Sequences - Short Stories Developing Generalizations

Pair up with another student with whom you think you can really talk. As your conversation progresses, stop at intervals to make <u>single sentence statements</u> about the most important things you are learning about one another's lives. After enough conversation for you to feel you know your partner quite well, study the statements you have made about him/her and try to identify the key quality or dominant factor in his/her life and state it as a <u>single sentence generalization</u>.

Now write a <u>short story</u> which develops this generalization and which finds your partner the main character in the story. Try to keep your partner's <u>personality</u> as true to real life as possible in the story you invent.

"Karen Burnett"

Generalization: Karen Burnett enjoys animals and sports and has a cheerful personality and an unyielding will.

Listen carefully and you can bet on the midnight ride of Karen Burnett.

Four score and seven years ago, Karen Burnett was one of the greatest jockeys that ever hit the trail. Horse fans would come from miles around just to see Karen mount the thoroughbred race horse that would be the first to cross the finish line.

These races were usually in favor of Karen, but on one particular day, the odds against her were almost insurmountable. The race was to take place on the Santa Anita race track, a fine but very slushy track for a hard rain had just hit. Along with its bad condition, the time scheduled for the race was twelve midnight, so danger of hurting the horse and jockey was tremendous.

"Bring your horses to the gate!" could be heard coming from the tall tower in the center of the racing area.

An instant later, Karen Burnett could easily be seen coming down the track because hundreds of bright lights lit it up. Karen's horse trotted into the starting stall, but now there was another factor against her and her horse. Although most horses had a good starting place and a light load, Karen's horse was in stall thirteen, second farthest from the rail, and it had a heavy load of 113 pounds. This just made Karen's desire to win stronger.

The horses panted and snorted nervously as they waited for their cue to dash onto the track and gain the rail.

The flag was down, and all the horses raced onto the track as if their lives depended on winning, but what really surprised the grandstand crowd was the fact that Karen Burnett held second to last place behind twelve other horses.

"Come on, Babe! The track is in bad condition, but pour on the steam, anyway! Let's show those other horses who's the best!" Karen whispered soothingly into the ear of her horse.

She lowered her head to meet almost ear to ear with the beast, gave it a light tap on the rump, and as if a bolt of lightning had struck him, the horse dashed towards the front to almost take first place.

"Just pass one more," Karen pleaded excitedly, "and we'll be in the lead!"

Once again, Karen and her horse bolted forward, this time to take the lead.

The many lights blinded Karen as she headed down the stretch, and the muddy track made it difficult for her horse to gain traction, but together they continued to hold the lead over the other exhausted horses. Soon, Karen and her powerful thoroughbred crossed the finish line first and the race was over. As if the crowd had known what the result would be all the time, it cheered with all its might. Karen just trotted away slowly and joked with all the other jockeys on her way, once again, to the winner's circle!

Maureen Donnels
Seventh Grade - 1969

Assignment 12 - Biographical Sequences -

True Autobiographical Sketches

Developing Generalizations

Reflect a bit on your own life and review important experiences you've had from as far back as you can remember until now. As you begin to identify key qualities which you think tend to make you the person you are, make <u>single sentence statements</u> and eventually a <u>single sentence generalization</u> about yourself. Now write a <u>true autobiographical sketch</u> which develops this generalization about yourself.

"Maureen Donnels"

Generalization: I enjoy meeting different people, going different places, trying different things, being athletic, making strong decisions, and having an optimistic attitude.

In this small world, there are many different types of people, each group having its own beliefs, religion, skin color, clothing, and other varying factors. Even within our own community, there are different people, rich men, poor men, happy men, sad men, etc., and each has a life of his own. Meeting different people can have many results. It can be educational or make you thankful for everything you have. Also, it can change your feelings or opinions. In addition, it can change your outlook on life.

You can also benefit by going different places. There are many different places to see, each captivating and holding its own secrets to be uncovered when explored. The lonely, barren but active desert is very different from a mountain peak covered with snow. There is always something new to see for our world is continually changing, and never could a person see everything.

Many writers write from experience, and many other things are done this way, also. Experience can be a basis for many things. As you try different things, you are gaining more and more experience. Some things have been proven unsafe and shouldn't be tried, but others should. Would Willie Mays be a famous baseball player if he hadn't ever tried to play baseball? When a person tries different things, he may find talents he may have otherwise never used. So, exploration into our world and the activities taking place in it can be very beneficial.

In addition to the above activities, I enjoy being athletic. This supposedly keeps me fit and in good health. Also, I enjoy doing most athletics or athletic sports. Sports and athletics have become very popular throughout the world, and for some sports, many new techniques of doing them have been developed.

I always try to make strong decisions. When I decide to do something, I usually do it. I have a strong mind, and I try not to let people influence my decisions. If I truly want to do something, no one is going to change my mind unless some good, concrete reasoning is presented why I shouldn't do it. Then, if I really decide not to, I won't

To conclude, I always try to be optimistic. I believe that if you truly believe in something, it has a very good chance of happening. So, if you want something to happen, you shouldn't tell yourself it won't. For example, yesterday when I was doing the high jump, instead of saying , "I'll never make it," I said, "I can do it, and I will!" and I did. So, if you are optimistic, life can be a lot easier.

Maureen Donnels
Seventh Grade - 1969

"Daryl Nelson"

Generalization: I try hard in school and sports, and do quite well in each.

First, let's take school. Many times I feel sorry for myself because I have so much schoolwork. But, I'm not like many other kids who say, "Ah, the heck with it!" and not do it at all. I take it as it is and try my best to complete it in the given time with the best possible workmanship. I would never "slough off" and take an "F" on a paper, even if it kept me up late at night perfecting a paper or rechecking a problem.

Even with two hours every week given to practicing my saxophone, and seven and a half to eight hours every week given to track or basketball practice, I think I do very well in school. Last report card I received 5 "A's" and 1 "B". I got the single "B" in spelling, but I still tried as hard as I could, and I'm proud of what I got.

In sports I try as hard as I do in my schoolwork. As I stated in the last paragraph, I usually devote about eight hours a week to sports. This year during basketball season my efforts paid off by earning me a starting forward position on the squad. Now, just these past two months, I've been involved in track. Each day I put my hard work into my field events. In the finals, I took a first in high jump and a fourth in the 440. I got thirty-five and a quarter points total in track and received a block in both track and basketball. Also, last year I gave up many hours of my summer vacation to become a member of the swim team. I've gotten several ribbons in this activity, also.

Altogether, I feel I am doing very good in school and sports. Of course, I could always do better. There is always room for improvement, and I hope I improve in sports and keep my grades up in school. I thank God for the wonderful talents He has given me, and I pray that I may continue using them to the best of my ability.

Daryl Nelson
Seventh Grade - 1969

Assignment 13 - Chronicles

Write a newspaper article designed to be published in a first-class junior high school newspaper. Write about events and ideas you think will <u>capture</u> a junior high school student's <u>attention</u>, and write with a style that'll hold their attention. Begin each article with a catchy title.

"Clowning around with Brown"

Did you ever stop to think about how our lives here at school are run by bells? True, we are also governed by the faculty, the administration and school rules, but when you are by the gym and have a class in room 26 with 30 seconds until bell-time, the bell is what's calling the shots. You can't run; that's against the school rules. So, in essence, we are trained to move when the bell rings.

Let's take a look at P.E. classes. Say you have P.E. third period. The bell at 11:00 a.m. rings; you go to P.E.; the bell at 11:05 a.m. rings; you should be in P.E.; the bell at 11:11 a.m. rings; you should be dressed down and standing on some number; the bell at 11:48 a.m. rings; that means get ready to get dressed; the bell at noon rings; it's lunch. That is five bells in one hour.

The bell system is working and has been working for hundreds of years, way back to the time when the teacher rang a little bell on her desk which meant silence, or when a big bell in the school yard would ring which meant that all little children should come to class.

But what if we didn't have bells? Would everything go as smoothly and as systematically as it does now? Or would things be utter chaos with students having no sense of time without looking at a clock? It's something to think about.

Tracey Brown
Ninth Grade - 1971

"Thoughts"

Why is it that most people seem to be so indifferent to each other? They seem to be living in their own separate world, everyone going their own way, not really caring what happens to anyone else as long as it doesn't concern them. There is never a friendly word or a smile for anyone because they are too concerned with their own little world. Some of them seem to be rude and uncaring. Can't people smile a little more and show a little more kindness and consideration for others? Instead of being burdened down all the time and preoccupied with their own thoughts, couldn't people try to be a little more caring sometimes and concern themselves with what is happening to everyone else in this world, or are they all too selfish?

There is much talk of peace and brotherhood, but is it just talk, or is it true to life? Are people really reaching out to one another with kindness? Many people are, but there are many who aren't. These are the people who are always pushing and shoving and stepping all over everyone to get someplace. They push and shove with never a word of regret or concern. This type of action I would not exactly call peaceful.

Why don't we all stop all our pushing and shoving and smile a little more and be more concerned with what is going on in the lives of others to prove that the idea of peace and brotherhood is not just words but true to life.

Randy Ryan
Ninth Grade - 1971

"Clowning around with Brown"

One day I was sick, so I stayed home from school and watched T.V. all day. The game shows in the morning were pretty good. I found out how much I didn't know.

But then came the stretch between noon and 2:00 p m. when your only choice was a soap opera. They were REALLY something!

64

I started watching one, exactly which one I don't know. Anyway, this girl and guy were running away to get married in some remote place. When they got to the Justice of the Peace, it was storming outside, so they couldn't go anywhere else. The guy was leaving for Viet Nam the next day, so they had to get married. By this time, I was just about ready to jump into the T.V. and marry them myself. The next thing I knew, they were flashing "The End" sign on the screen.

I turned the channel, and there was another soap opera. This time it was about a crazy lady who took her sister's baby and took off. She was driving on roads that only Superman should attempt. She finally got to a motel that a little old man owned. By the time it was over, I thought for sure I had an ulcer.

But not all soap operas are bad. The kind I like are where John Doe's wife is in love with Sarah Doolittle's husband. In the meantime Sarah Doolittle is in love with Joe Schmoe. But Joe Schmoe's wife is in love with John Doe, who is in love with Mary Doe (John Doe's wife) even though she hates his guts. Then John Doe dies, so Mary Doe kills Sarah Doolittle so she can have her husband. Then when Sarah Doolittle is on her death bed, Sam Doolittle (Sarah Doolittle's husband) finds out that Sarah was in love with Joe Schmoe, so he goes and kills Joe Schmoe. Then, just so it wouldn't appear as if she were happy, Gertrude Schmoe kills Sam Doolittle. Mary Doe gets mad at Gertrude Schmoe , so she kills Gertrude. Then at the end, Mary Doe ends up marrying Sam Doolittle's brother. All of the soap operas don't have such easy plots.

The thing that makes me really mad with the soap operas is that they always put a commercial on when it's at a good part. George Handsome will be down on his knees, asking for forgiveness, while Nancy Beautiful will be sitting on a couch crying her dear heart out. Then the famous words come: George says, "Nancy, will you marry ?"

Nancy balls up her fist and begins to say, "Oh . . ." COMMERCIAL TIME.

I come back to reality just to find myself down on the floor about to propose to a chair. Those "soapies" can really get to you.

Next time you have a spare half hour, watch a soap opera. You never know,you may end up trying to drive your refrigerator.

Tracey Brown
Ninth Grade - 1972

"Mission Suicide"

Every day I get bruised, mangled, tripped, pushed, shoved, elbowed, and socked while going through E-Hall in a sea of people struggling for their lives.

Now, I'm sure everyone has gone through the hassle of trying to get through the E-Hall; it's virtually impossible. It's even worse when you fall and are lying half-dead on the ground and some nut says, "Excuse you!" while he is putting his footprint in your back.

At this point, one thing comes into play, MANNERS. It's evident that most people's manners can be termed as "Bad". Maybe I shouldn't knock them so hard; maybe they don't know that it is bad manners to say, "Excuse you!" to a person whose spinal cord they are mutilating.

Once every three months, two weeks, four days, five hours, and 23.42 minutes the E-Hall will have only a half million people in it instead of the whole million. You are breathing freely when all of a sudden something hits you in the back; you hit the person in front of you in the back; they hit the person in front of them in the back, and it becomes a chain reaction. The poor person in the front gets trampled to death. What happened? Some freak of nature decided to come charging through the hall.

Now that I have complained about the conditions, I guess I should offer a suggestion to solve them. I know that there is no cure for the crowds in the halls, but how about MANNERS? A little common courtesy never hurt anyone. Next time you cut someone, offer them a band aid; next time you trample someone, help them up. You never know, they may help you one day.

Tracey Brown
Ninth Grade - 1972

"The Rincon Rush"

Before we realize it, the end of the quarter will pounce upon us like a lion waiting for its prey. Suddenly, three-fourths of the students will be thrown into a desperate panic , struggling to bring up their grades at the last minute. The much dreaded report cards will be out, and what the students and their parents see may be upsetting.

This is all unnecessary and could be simply and completely avoided. This means cracking the books now and taking school seriously for a change. After all, school is one of the most important times of your life, whether you realize it or not. School, especially junior and senior high school, pretty much decides your entire future. It can decide whether or not you can win a scholarship, whether or not you will go to college, what you'll be doing for a living, and how much money you will earn. Is it really worth it to throw it all away? And for what? A few kicks? A good time? Take the time to look at yourself and your future.

My statements are based upon fact. In a few days, or so, you'll notice it, also. The scramble for books, reports, and projects will be unbelievable. This panic is something that occurs often during the school year. How Rincon survives it is a question I have been asking myself for a long time, but I still haven't found the answer to it.

It never fails. Two days before the end of the quarter, students flock to the library study area in atrocious numbers, trying to make up those much needed extra credit points in an impossible amount of time. Countless hours are spent late at night in a frantic rush to read the book that is due the next morning.

Take it easy. Avoid the rush and confusion. Get busy now and sit back and sigh later. After all, what can you lose?

Brian Bartlett
Ninth Grade - 1976

Assignment 14 - Short Histories

Title the first history you write, "Junior High and I," and write an account of your junior high school experiences up to the present time. Near the end of this history make some judgments about how your junior high school experience has affected you and what you liked and disliked about it. Also, if you wish, try to project yourself into your future school years and predict what kinds of changes you will make in your life.

Can you think of other short histories that'd be fun to write?

"Junior High and I"

I changed the most in my life so far during this school year. I matured, and more and more responsibilities were put on me. There was more work and more learning happening than before. Even with the added work laid on me, seventh grade has been a most interesting and exciting year of life.

I changed the most this year because of this school. The teachers expected more out of me, and they expected me to act better. During the first quarter, teachers took it easy with me, but for the rest of the year they really cracked down, and I learned a lot.

In this process I grew not only physically, but mentally. I can see now, looking back at sixth grade, how childish things were. I played silly tricks on substitutes and beat up little kids. The teachers didn't help me grow. They let me go after I did something wrong. They gave me too much freedom and then expected me to use it wisely. If they had wanted me to learn more, they should have cracked down with more discipline. When I came to seventh grade, in P.E. I got to play games like killer ball, caveman basketball, and soccer and to wrestle. In sixth grade our principal wouldn't let us play ball tag because we threw the ball too hard. The reason I think I changed so much was because of discipline.

I can easily see how I changed during the first semester of this school year. I can remember when there used to be a fight on our block how I used to go see it to see who won. Now, I go to a fight to break it up. I do this by asking questions like, "Why are you fighting?"

One of the fighters usually says, "He threw the ball at me!"

Another fighter says, "I did not!"

I say, "Big deal! It was an accident. Shake hands and play some more baseball."

In the second semester, I changed even more. I began seeing why I should like girls. Girls were not cootie freaks anymore. I learned about love. I began to feel the creativeness about writing and how to make math fun.

I began opening my mind, seeing what was happening in this world. I began to open myself to other people and tell them what was inside me. I also discovered what was happening with other people. The average and below average people were like outsiders, so they joined a group of people. And to stay in their group, they had to do what the group did, and that was smoke, take drugs, and that stuff. I began to see what was happening to those people. They started rebelling about learning, they hated school, and they couldn't wait to get out. I can see in the future what's going to happen to them. It makes me sad to see what they're missing.

During seventh grade many responsibilities were put on me. Around the second quarter I could feel the pressure from what was expected of me. I also felt the pressure of getting good grades. At first I asked myself this question, "Is this what it's like to grow up?" By the third quarter I began to enjoy life more because what my parents hadn't let me do before, they began letting me do now. I've discovered how much responsibility will be on me as I grow up.

In the past year I've learned a lot and changed a lot. I've changed from the first day of school this year 'til right now. It's been a short time, a year, but I've changed a lot. I've never before told about or written so much about what's inside of me. I've never before let myself go like this, but it feels good.

See that! I changed right there! I think I'm going to open myself up like this again soon.

Jack Deibert
Seventh Grade - 1975

"Junior High and I"

I was finally going to be a seventh grader in junior high school. I was excited, but, in a way, scared to death! My sisters and other people had told me stories about how people got initiated on the first day of school, and also that in P.E. you had to take a shower in open showers. I was surprised when none of this was true. (Except some of the boys did get initiated.)

After about a month, it was strange to think that we now hated some of the girls we had been hanging around with last year. Elections for class officers came around, and I ran for vice-president and lost. But that's not what got the best of me. The girl who made it was very stuck up, pretty, and an enemy of mine! I still say her looks won it. That passed, and the play came around. I was in orchestra, but I hated it and wanted to be in the play rather than play the piano. So, I got stuck as the curtain puller!

In eight grade I started realizing how much competition and favoritism there was in our school. This I didn't like at all! First of all, I got stuck in a P.E. class with only one of my friends, and then she broke her leg and was out for the year. I made friends with a lot of ninth graders. I tried out for cheerleading but didn't make it. Neither did the girl I tried out with. A lot of people said that both of us should have made it. I also learned that the guys liked the girls for their good looks. That really got the best of me! So, it came time for the play again, and I tried out for a lead part. Again I didn't make it. It was disappointing but not terribly upsetting because there was always next year to get a part.

I thought I would have a fairly good chance. On the last day of school it was kinda upsetting because most of my graduating ninth grade friends would probably not be seeing me very much because of the grade difference.

They all told me how great ninth grade would be and how fast it would go by. It did go fast, but everything was a let down. I tried out for cheerleading again and lost again! This time it really upset me because I wanted it so bad. I still wasn't over this when the play came around. Ninth grade was different from what I expected. It was my worst grade in junior high. Especially when

I tried out for the lead in the play again and didn't make it. I thought I deserved it more than anyone else.

The three years I spent in junior high were very disappointing and not happy, but if I had given up like I nearly decided to do, I wouldn't be a sophomore cheerleader now!

Linda Jennings
Ninth Grade - 1978

Assignment 15 - Short Stories

Write a short story about a <u>real experience</u> you've had. Try to <u>recreate</u> every detail exactly as it happened, even telling how you felt when it happened. As you write your story, keep asking yourself this question, "Will the person who reads this be able to <u>relive</u> my experience?" Keep working at it until your answer is "Yes!"

Character, dialogue, plot, setting, and theme are <u>all</u> essential elements of a good story. They're words which identify what you'll be doing when you make a serious effort at <u>recreating</u> one of your <u>real</u> experiences for others to <u>relive</u>. You'll be putting <u>people</u> in <u>action</u> at a certain <u>time</u> and <u>place</u>, and you'll be creating the <u>words they say</u>! You'll be sharing an experience from which others can <u>learn</u>. What they learn is what your experience <u>teaches</u>. That's <u>theme</u>.

After you've successfully written a real experience, let your imagination run wild and <u>invent</u> a <u>fictional experience</u>. The <u>trick</u> is to be able to make what you haven't personally experienced seem so real that your reader won't know the difference. Sometimes, this can involve researching for facts before you begin or as you proceed so that what you are writing rings true.

"Poppy"

Usually, that name means one of two things to people, an important and delicate flower or something very bouncy, even noisy. To me it was a majestic, loving, shepherd, a golden dog, not in color, but in being. I loved that dog!

How inadequate that sounds, how positively naked and barren. Like a pair of pantaloons, it might look better with ruffles to cover up the rawness, but then it would not express the depth and beauty with which I "loved" her; that combination of guttural sounds, like a lock, opens to display the wealth of the word.

Poppy came to me at three months of age, shivering, skinny, and with that stigma of curly fur so scorned when found on a shepherd. Mr. Groves, an important man at Guide Dogs for the Blind, San Rafael, California, brought the dog to my house. She had thrown up on the way down and was positively repulsive looking. Nevertheless, I loved her on sight. Perhaps because we both had curly hair, perhaps because we both got carried away with things, or perhaps because sitting there she struck a responsive chord in my well-hidden, and as of yet decidedly small, motherly nature.

I spent a year of my life with her, loving her, training her, scolding her. So much of what we did together is now irreplaceable, beautiful and gone forever. In a fast game of tetherball, she was an avid player, throwing the ball with her snout and front paws; water skiing, she would watch anxiously out of the back of the boat, my falling making her go into hysterics. Sitting on a dewy lawn before a field day at 5:30 in the morning, listening to the crickets, I would fall asleep to the monotonous drone of her doggy snore, only to have to wake up and rouse her from a nightmare. Eighteen months I trained her: heel, sit, stay, come, down, and fetch, rescuing Easter eggs and Christmas decorations from her.

Finally, the day came. Mr. Groves drove up and bore away one bewildered shepherd. With the certainty of love, I knew she would not be accepted (given to a blind person) or in other words separated from me. Two, four, six months passed, and the hopeful, fearful feeling that she would be accepted grew. I tried to act like I didn't care, and failed. It would have been a masterful bit of hypocrisy. One day I returned home from school only to have my mother tell me she had been accepted. How noble I was; the glory, the prestige, my first dog accepted, and a hard to handle shepherd. Elevated on a bubble of self-esteem, I did not fall to earth until we arrived at San Rafael for the graduation.

I wasn't sure she'd remember me. How ashamed I am to recall this. I entered the room, admiring but failing to recognize my own dog. Large, black and silver, she leapt on me. I had had my stomach steeled for a blank look of unrecognition. My self-control gone, I knelt and held her and cried! An elderly man fought to control her as we leapt together in wild abandon.

The blind man and I talked. His name was Mr. Center, Poppy's new owner. All sorts of thoughts filled my mind. Was he kind to her? Did he take good care of her? Above all, could he give her the love she required? He could, but still I felt a painful nagging at my heart as I mentally attempted to disengage myself from her and emulate the stoic attitude of the blind man in front of me. It was the nagging of jealousy and selfishness. But he was not stoic; no, he cried, too, perhaps because with the sensitivity cultivated by the blind, he felt my pain.

We sat a little uncomfortably, gently glad when the lunch bell rang, and he had to go. My nobility gone, I was simply sad that I was losing a dog. I was pleased though. If I dropped dead, somebody would have profited by my existence. I had "carved my niche in the edifice of society," done my thing. Mr. Center got up with Poppy and walked away. She kept looking back, and he had to jerk her to go forward.

They say the heart has many chambers. Well, the supports for one of my chambers collapsed, and it fell in when she walked out.

I stood outside and watched Mr. Center sit down to eat, downing Poppy at his feet. Poppy got a glimpse of me and rose to her feet, but at a command from Mr. Center, she lay . . ., and in that moment, I lost her.

The sun was setting. It came down over everything, the skiing, the tetherball games, the moonlit mornings, the snores. In the immortal, if not modified, words of somebody's, "It was a far, far better thing I did than I have ever done for the elements were so mixed in her that all my being might stand up and say, 'This was a dog!'"

Kim Haylock
Eighth Grade - 1970

"To Be Wild"

We lived in a small apartment in Brussels, Belgium, a small home where my family had stayed for several months, a place to rest and keep away from the squeezed, overcrowded life of the metropolis. It was owned by a rich, middle-aged landlady, Madame Lebrun, who lived in the second story with her husband and only daughter, Cynthia. The place was well-furnished with a large, glass table in the dining room where I would do my homework at night. We ate in the kitchen, the warmest room of the apartment, where we could gather together to talk of our different adventures of the day.

But outside our kitchen door was the area I had loved so much, the area where my story takes place. It was a large garden surrounded by a high stone wall, the house and refuge of several animals, a hiding place from the polluted environment of the city. It was a beautiful area, always fresh and verdant from the rainy weather, carpeted with ground moss and wild blossoms from which sprang two large poplar trees stretching out and sheltering the many birds that came to nest in their tangled branches.

It was late in the afternoon when the bird fell. It came down, tumbling wildly from its nest perched up high in the tree, and landed on the carpet of moss and grass beneath it. My younger sister, Sheila, was the first to notice. She was a young girl, aged five, with all the fresh, energetic curiosity of all young children. "David!" she cried. "A bird fell from the tree!"

I was sitting at the dining room table, completing my homework, papers and folders scattered in all directions. I turned around in my chair.

"A what?"

"A bird!" There was a look of excitement on her face as she pointed out the window. I ran towards it and looked outside. It lay on the ground, hopping wildly about and fluttering its wings.

"Let's go get it!" she cried

She grabbed my hand eagerly as we set out for the kitchen door. We entered the garden and ran to the foot of the tree. It was a small, baby bird, hopping about on one foot, the other torn and bleeding. Its wing was also badly damaged and fell limply to its side while the bird beat the other furiously, desperately trying to fly back to its nest.

"What should we do?" Sheila asked me, looking up to me with large, inquisitive eyes.

"Pick it up, I guess," I said. She released my hand and stepped back, fixing her gaze on the injured bird as I reached out my hands to touch it as it rested up for another struggle. I closed my fingers securely around it and picked it up. It gave out a cry of pain as it struggled to be released from my grasp. It was warm, its heart beating rapidly, as I cautiously carried it to the kitchen. Sheila came up close to watch, fixing her large eyes on it.

It was a small baby dove, covered with a fresh, white coat of feathers, carefully preened by its mother. I walked slowly through the door and carried it inside. It was warm in the kitchen, the stove burning on the other side of the room. I set the bird gently on the table and walked to the sink to get some water. I filled a small glass from the cupboard and set it on the table. I lifted the bird and lowered its tiny, pointed, orange beak into the water. Sheila was watching all the time, on tip-toe, as the bird stood there, poised, beak in the glass, and I waited for it to drink. It seemed to be frozen in my hands, immobile. I felt the beating of its heart and the warmth radiating from its small body into my hands as the room held its breath. It was silent, tense, Sheila peering anxiously at the head poised above the water.

"It isn't drinking," she said. A feeling of frustration came over me as I stood and waited.

"Don't worry," I said. "It will."

"But it isn't!"

I lifted the bird and set it on the table. I looked it over with anxious eyes, trying to discover what was keeping it from drinking, but found nothing. I lifted it again and lowered its beak a second time into the glass, still not understanding why the wild bird refused to drink. I gave up a few minutes later, confused and frustrated by a bird for which I had the highest hopes, but which would not take anything from me. Why wouldn't it accept my offerings?

I left the table and walked away. A few minutes later I returned with a small shoebox stuffed with cotton and rags, ready for another try with the water. No matter how hard I prayed, waited, or used force, it wouldn't drink a thing. It would only stay poised there stupidly while I forced its beak into the water. I was confused and bewildered. I had no knowledge of wild animals and birds. In my young life, I had only known domesticated pets, those associated with the human world. An animal, for me, was a plaything, a relation, a being that I could take care of, something that I could trust and with which I could live. But this bird was only a source of frustration for me, a being that refused all my love and attention.

Mother walked into the room and set a bag of groceries noisily on the kitchen counter. She did not see my patient as she walked in, but turned around to notice it. I hadn't the faintest idea of being discovered, and here I was, standing in front of the table, the bird tucked away in the box. I placed it behind my back as Sheila quickly ducked under the table, ready for another scolding session to take place. Mother stood in front of me, hands on her hips.

"What are you hiding?"

I squeezed uncomfortably against the table and gripped the box in my hands.

"Nothing, Mother."

She didn't look satisfied.

"Mother, please! I don't have anything, honest! I . . . "

In one swift, deft movement she shot out her hand and grabbed the box. A look of compassion came over her face as she held it and looked inside. The bird was carefully tucked in rags, covered with several handkerchiefs and a pillow under its head. She stood facing me and looked me straight in the eye. Then came the fateful words.

"You can't take care of it inside."

"But, Mother!" I cried. "It'll freeze out there!"

"But you don't understand . . ."

"Yes, I do! You want the bird to freeze!"

"Calm down," she said. She sat me down and explained.

"This bird is wild, David. It won't survive in here."

"Mother, it'll freeze outside!"

"Birds are used to it. They live outside. It will die in here."

I refused to listen. I turned away and closed my ears. She stood up, sighed, and quietly brought the box outside the kitchen. I ran after her. She stopped and grabbed me firmly by the shoulders.

"You have to keep it outside."

"Mother, no!" I tore myself from her grasp and ran for the box. I secured my hands around it and brought it to my room, locking the door behind me. I was frustrated, angry, and confused. I looked at the bird, now lying silently in the box. Its eyes had lost their glaze, the lids had closed over them, and its wings were badly swollen at the joints. I hesitated. I looked out the window upon the garden and the large tree that spread out before me. A nest lay in one of the branches, swaying gently in the wind. I looked around my room, the lamp, closet and bed, the walls that enclosed the place. It was compact, tight, compared to the spacious free area that lay beyond the window. It was jostling, alive, not prefabricated with dead materials. The bird was a creature born to live in a free environment, born to be wild.

I brought it down the stairs and placed it outside. I was uncertain, afraid, unsure of my mother's words, but something told me that she was right.

That night I brought the box inside to feed the bird. Father was there to help me, waiting with a bowl of bread crumbs soaked in milk. The bird was pale now, wan looking, its feathers disheveled and gray. We tried to feed it with a matchstick, slowly pushing food down its throat. It would only take a little at a time, swallowing slowly. We gave it as much food as we could, and I brought it back outside.

There were no stars, the sky was clouded overhead, and I could hear the faint, distant rumbling of thunder. I hesitated and then placed the bird gently on the ground.

Dinner was silent. I was thinking of the bird all the time, lying in its box. Sheila was silently praying by herself, having forgotten about it. I sat on the couch and stared into the blazing fire, flickering and dancing. Confusion, anger, and hope were all choked up in me as I sat thinking. I was scared.

I went to bed late that night after trying to feed the bird a second time, and I lay awake for an hour, listening to the faint rumbling of thunder playing with the trees. Lying silently, I drifted to sleep, dreaming of the bird, its coat of feathers a dazzling white, its eyes a glossy black, flying back to its nest in the brilliant green branches.

I awoke in the middle of the night, rain beating on the window. Thunder was shaking the windows, together with the bright yellow flashes of lightning. I felt sweaty and uncomfortable in my bed, uneasy and frightened. The thought of the bird sent a lightening bolt down my spine.

I scrambled out of my bed and tiptoed down the stairs into the kitchen. It was dark and cold, the fire in the living room only a pile of dying embers. A thunderclap exploded and shook the window, followed with a bright flash of lightning. I was trembling. I approached the kitchen door slowly and grasped the doorknob. The door flung open, and a large gust of wind swept me into the beating rain. I groped around in the dark, searching and calling out. A black shape emerged a few feet ahead of me. I grabbed it. It was the box, but empty. I looked around, hoping to find some trace of the bird. A shadow stood a few feet before me. I looked at it, unbelieving. A flash of lightning illuminated the yard. I saw it lying before me, in the pale yellow light, dead! A chill of terror went down my spine while I stood in the downpour, unbelieving, frightened.

I dashed through the door and ran up the stairs into my parents' room. My father turned on the lamp to find me standing sopping wet before him. Confusion and terror were all mixed up inside me and came out in long, hysterical sobs.

"What's going on?" he asked.

"It died!" I cried. "It's dead!"

We held the funeral that morning under the tree, with a small procession of children. The sky had cleared, and the sun was shining through, the garden still as alive as ever. I found the bird lying on the ground in a puddle of water, its head turned to the side and its feet sticking up in the air. I picked it up and placed it in a shoebox and called the children around the neighborhood for a funeral procession. It was a solemn one, I standing by the grave as Father read from an old Bible. I left after a half an hour and walked back into the kitchen. I looked out the window upon the old stone wall. Two birds, a couple, sat perched upon it, calling out for their lost, dead child. I wanted to yell to them, "It's dead! It's gone! Over with!" But I knew they wouldn't understand. Wild will never mean the same to me again, and the word "wild" will always remind me of the painful and emotional experience that led me to its meaning.

David Jager
Seventh Grade - 1981

"The Death of Butter"

Here I rest, alone and dismal, in a butter dish on a mahogany table, awaiting calmly a fateful demise. Grace is solemnized, and the Adams family of six settles down for its leisurely evening meal. A dull implement is thrust into my side, and I am lifted high above the table and transported towards a plate. Suddenly, I fall, and a shriek reaches my ears, "Jo Anne, why can't you be more careful? See that mark the butter has made on the tablecloth!"

My trip is continued until at last I reach the craterous valley in Jo Anne's potatoes. I am extremely comfortable, for my resting place is warm, so different from my previous refrigerator home. Ah! What luxury! Such comfort!

Now, Jo Anne is taking me for a ride around my valley. It's fun for awhile, but now I'm becoming dizzy, and I wish Jo Anne would cease my ride. Suddenly, I know that this is done in order that I might melt faster. Do humans only think of themselves?

My flesh is softening, and many unconnected thoughts race through my mind. I remember my refrigerator friends, a jovial lot of apples and a merry bunch of tomatoes. I recall many joyful adventures. How I wish I still resided in my old abode.

My blood envelops me; my heart begins to weaken. In a matter of seconds I will be nothing but liquid flavoring. My last thought harps on my mind. Humans are murderers! Humans are murderers!

Candy Bell
Seventh Grade - 1961

"Algebra Island"

Amid the Sea of Imagination and in the Realm of Curiosity, there lies an island neither large nor small, but infinitely just so. It is called Algebra Island, and quite appropriately named, I would say.

The inhabitants of this island are letters, ordinary letters like A, B, C, D, etc. And it is quite natural that these letters should have children, the little letters, a, b, c, d, etc.

Now, of course, the little letters mature and enter that despairing period of adulthood known as Pronumerality where they are faced with the groping problem of discovering their true identity and purpose in life. Some letters prefer to remain indolent, so do not even attempt to make their lives worthwhile or profitable. These torpid letters are shunned by all as outcasts and are compelled to forever remain unknowns! However, the more ambitious, determined letters resolutely journey to the Land of Roots by way of the Road of Solution where they should discover themselves.

The Road of Solution is a winding path that twists and turns and dips and climbs endlessly where one meets obstacles that ironically aid the clever or lucky letter in his search.

The first obstacle a letter is confronted with is the Bridge of Understanding. This Bridge is composed of thousands and thousands of pieces of tiny gray rope loosely tied together in knots. So wobbly and shaky is it that some letters fall from the Bridge and plunge below into the Whirlpool of Confusion.

No sooner do the letters cross the Bridge than before them haughtily towers the Mathematical Pyramid, a labyrinthine maze, intricately designed! Some letters have no difficulty in finding their way out of the maze. Some have a great deal of difficulty. And some never do find the correct passage which will lead them out of the pyramid. These letters are always searching and forever roaming through the various passages of the Mathematical Pyramid, but always these passages lead them to dead ends where the letters must turn and start anew, tirelessly attempting to find their way out.

Finally, the letters can see their destination. On top of a mountain (called The Mountain for no better name has been found for it), they see the Land of Roots. They vigorously, earnestly climb The Mountain. Some fall in the process of doing so, but others continue. And then they reach their goal, The Land of Roots. And suddenly they realize everything -- that they're numbers -- ordinary numbers like 1, 2, 3, 4, etc. And here most stay; however, a few lose their bearing and tumble down The Mountain, never to return to its top again. But most stay on the top of The Mountain and lead prosperous and fruitful lives filled with happiness and contentment. How I wish all letters could live atop The Mountain!

Susan Peabody
Seventh Grade - 1961

"Confessions of a Thanksgiving Day Meal"

Dawn was just breaking when the lights in the Big House snapped on. The world was still plunged in the blackness of pre-morning when the cattle scrambled to their feet, lowing softly to the rest of the barnyard life, awakening Chanticleer himself.

He flapped swiftly away with short, powerful beats of his wings against the air and landed on the weathercock. He screamed like a banshee, and the noise brought the weary animals to their feet, and they milled sleepily about.

The sun's brightness grew, and its head peeped up above the distant hills, as if timidly awaiting a signal to rise farther. Long, black shadows were cast over the yard as a dim figure emerged from the house, a lantern held high, and in front of it shooting thin, pale streaks into the gray mist.

The animals recognized the slow shuffling steps of the farmer and disappeared into the shadows, as specters descending into eternal gloom.

I crouched down under the security of the fence, dreading his appearance. My fellow pigs could not contain their fear, and they expressed themselves in thin little squeaks. Their brown and white spotted hides heaved and trembled in terror, and the barnyard became suddenly quiet.

The footsteps crunched stealthily nearer on the gravel near our pen. I quickly changed my position to face in that direction, and the lantern suddenly went out.

There was only profound silence. Not a thing moved, nor did the breeze stir the treetops. I felt like squealing, but in my terror I could not. Riveted to the spot, I listened with all senses alert, my stubbly ears pricked up, and my eyes straining to detect the slightest movement.

Suddenly, the farmer made a careless move and uttered an oath. He stumbled and crashed to the ground inside the pen, and the lantern tinkled musically as it smashed against the fence. He reached out an arm in a lightning-quick motion and grabbed my hind legs. I was captured!

I squealed in terror all the way to the Big House and received several rough cuffs because of this. The farmer shuffled into the house and pinned me down on a table covered with newspapers. His roly-poly wife brought him something sharp and polished. Something was going to happen to me! But What?

Silence filled the quaint, little kitchen. The farmer stood above me, his face cold and impassive, and with an almost wicked gleam in his eye, the Thing upraised in his hand.

The arm lifted into the air and held there a moment before it came whistling down towards me, slicing the air with a swooshing sound. And then all was blackness.

It had been after this terrible chopping that I was shoved into a red-hot oven. For five hours I lay thus, roasting in the little box, feeling quite hot under the collar. Then the door creaked open on its hinges, and a fat, jolly face thrust itself through the opening, as a castle drawbridge would descend, and a merry knight would enter, bent on conquest.

I was carefully removed, placed in a sizzling pan, and stuffed uncomfortably with various kinds of dressings, crumbled breads, and chopped vegetables.

I was then conveyed into an old-fashioned room with a large table in the middle of the floor and eight chairs around it. Several pieces of chinaware hung on the walls, and the silverware was shined to perfection.

A soft, yellow tablecloth encompassed the length of the table, and it was upon this that I was delicately placed with several varieties of dishes, meats, and vegetables about me.

The aroma of fresh corn that sat next to me, as if sharing with me this strange, new experience, was a familiar smell. People began to rush back and forth from the dining room to the kitchen and back again, carrying huge plates of steaming food: spaghetti, tamales, hors d'oeuvres, meat loaf, and greased pans of yellow rolls with butter dripping down the sides of them.

As the people continued to rush madly about, clattering plates and pans, chattering and jabbering good-naturedly in the full joy of the holiday and generally making themselves a nuisance, a group of us engaged in conversation.

"Wot Luck!" raved the English muffin. "Here we sit, unmindful of all the things that go on in our world, broiled, baked, cut, chopped, shredded, rolled, plastered, burned, and scared half to death by these carnivorous savages, carefully prepared for human consumption! This is sacrifice, that's what it is! Rot!" He wiped away the sticky butter that dripped into his eye.

"You think you have something to gripe about, eh?" snarled the French hors d'oeuvre at his age old enemy. "Ma foi! I've had my skin constantly pricked with stabbing toothpicks at the pleasure of . . . of these beasts!"

"Whoa, fellows," I broke in. "I was just about to say --" and I was rudely interrupted by the Italian.

"Mama Mia!" yelled the spaghetti. "I have been scalded and plastered with sauce on this day as none of you nor the American have been treated!"

"Why, you dirty swine!" snapped the American meatloaf in reply. "All you Nazis are--" and he uttered a vehement oath, one which I had better not relate here.

"Look," I interposed, "this is not World War II." But the tamales roared into action.

"Por Dios!" roared the Mexican in surprise. "My mother country, Spain, fought nobly in the Spanish-American War and almost licked this peasant's country," pointing to meatloaf, "except for--" and he stated a reason, provoking the whole group to blast into raving fits, yells, and arguments.

They all quieted, however, when the Thanksgiving grace was said. Someone muttered, "Fall to!" and the forks clattered and everything was passed around.

I was one of the first to go. A sharp five-pronged instrument came for me and caught me up. I dangled there on the end of the fork, a helpless slab of hot bacon in the air. And then I was rushing toward a cavernous hole with the speed of the wind.

I spun around and around, and felt like screaming, but I could not. The hole closed over me, and pearly-white gates barred my way.

The set wall of razor-sharp whiteness opened to admit me, but before I could pass through, I was swiftly crushed and ground into small particles. Something pulled me down, down, and suddenly there was a sharp drop.

I plunged into space, the walls of the esophagus tube enclosing me. I slid down for what seemed a mile when I heard a strange hissing sound, and digestive juices pounded into me and forced me into the stomach.

It churned me into pulp, adding saliva to my body as a wash-day miracle soap would be added to the machine.

Ground into even smaller bits, I zoomed into the liver and then the pancreas, receiving a supply of saliva for use in the small intestines. The bile made in the liver was stored in the gall bladder through which I passed as if I was a wayfarer passing through a city.

Incredibly tiny particles made up my body now as I edged my way into the duodenum, and then flowed freely into the small intestines. I began to feel myself separating as I neared the "Red Sea."

And then I was caught up in a mass of blood and propelled downstream as surely as an Indian paddles his canoe down a great current. I was swished into the current and dissolved, and then rushed on and away into the unknown.

Rick Delanty
Eighth Grade - 1964

84

"Victory"

Victory Benneker was at the sixth grade ice-skating and dancing party. An unpopular, nobody boy asked Victory to dance.

"Well, do you want to dance or not?" he asked.

"I guess I will," she replied.

As Victory and the boy began to dance, Victory tripped over her feet and clumsily tumbled to the floor. The next thing she knew the nobody boy was yelling at her while a crowd of kids watched.

"What a clutz you are! One simple, little, easy dance and you mess it all up by tripping all over yourself, and from what I saw, your skating wasn't that hot either!"

Earlier in the evening, Victory was on the ice rink, skating around, trying to be as graceful as she could possibly be. She was concentrating so much on her gracefulness that she wasn't aware of a boy coming her way. Well, they ended up bumping into each other. Victory was so startled by this happening that she burst into tears and cried out bitterly, "I'm always messing up at things!" A few kids yelled some snide remarks:

"That's true!"

"Yeah, it is! I guess you don't measure up to your name anymore, Victory!"

After the mess-ups Victory had, she went home.

The next day after school, Victory slowly trudged into the living room of her house and plopped herself into an easy chair.

"Hi, Victory! How was school today?"

"Oh, hi, Mom. I guess it was okay."

"You don't sound very enthused. Are you sure something isn't wrong?"

"Well, we held class elections today. I ran for president."

"I can tell by your face that you didn't win. Well, what did you get instead, secretary, treasurer, class guard, what?"

"None of 'em. I only got six votes, but I did get a part in the sixth grade class play about pollution."

Victory's mother's eyes beamed with pleasure. "What are the parts and props?"

"Four litterers, five old pieces of junk, smog, erosion, noise, and a little boy."

"I'll bet you get one of the lead parts."

"No, I got the part of a can!"

"That isn't bad. At least you'll be seen."

"Nope, I won't! I'll be floating, almost sinking, in a lake, and I have only three lines!"

"Well, dear, why don't you watch T.V. while I fix dinner."

"I'll just sit here and wait, Mom."

"Well, dear, if that's what you want, but don't plop on the chair anymore."

"Yeah, okay."

Victory's mother walked out of the room and turned the corner into the kitchen, a look of puzzlement and disappointment written all over her face. Victory sat in the chair, staring at the ceiling, as she slowly dozed off and began dreaming . . .

"We return once again to your emcee for the evening, Jerry Jordan:

Hello, again, folks! The moment you have all been waiting for is here. We're ready to announce the winner of the 1975 Miss Beauty Queen Contest. The final votes of the judges have been tallied. May I have the envelope please! And the winner is . . . Miss Victory Benneker! Victory, would you please . . .."

"Victory, Victory!" Victory's ears perked up.

"Did you say something, Mom?"

"Victory, you've been dreaming again. It's dinner time."

The rest of the evening went well. Two weeks of dreaming and clumsiness passed rapidly for Victory and led to the night of the play and Victory's scene. The spotlight focused on the lake, Beer Can Victory dimly shining in the carbon paper water. Tension slowly pulsed through her, her single line about to be spoken.

"And I, a beer can, tossed to my death, am slowly sinking. Oh, no, the lake, I ripped it!"

Roars of laughter rippled throughout the crowd as a voice sounded above the rest.

"Have you forgotten your name's Victory?"

The next morning Victory was caught dreaming in her English class, but lucky for her it was near the end of the class. Before the shrill bell rang, Victory heard the teacher's voice fade in, "So, for tomorrow, class, I would like you to write a story. It may be fictitious or true. It may even be pure fantasy. Victory was looking at the chalkboard when she glanced down at her desk and saw a note from her best friend, Cheryl, which read, "Hey, Vicky, is anything wrong? Write back."

Victory's note answered, "Kinda. I'm always messing up at things. I don't fit my name too well. Plus, I'm always dreaming."

Cheryl wrote back, "Yeah, I heard about what happened in the English class this morning. What was the dream about?"

Victory replied, "Well, this girl, supposedly me, was really pretty and popular. She had the longest blonde hair imaginable and was super smart, so smart that she won a trip around the world. It had stuff about what happened about the trip."

Cheryl wrote, "I've got a theory. Maybe your dreams are a gift. Why don't you use 'em wisely. Every time you have one, write it down and turn it into a story. Then turn in the stories.

Victory began taking Cheryl's advice, and it worked. One morning Victory's teacher called her up to her desk for a private conference. "Vicky, your writing has suddenly become better than excellent! That's what this conference is about. In the junior high you'll be entering, there is a special journalism class for students who may be able to have a career as writers."

"Me?"

"Yes. This class is only for the top writers, and I showed the teacher a sample of your writing."

Victory spoke with enthusiasm and yet she was hesitant, "Uh, what happened?"

"She said you'd fit in perfectly. That is, if you'd like to enter that class instead of English."

"Yes! Yes, I would! Thank you! Thanks so much!"

"You're quite welcome, Vicky."

Giving a full-length, cheerful smile, Victory said, "I'd prefer to be called 'Victory'."

Laura Christensen
Seventh Grade - 1975

"Television's Revenge"

Mrs. Morris flew out of the room in a flurry, her eyes filled with terror! She raced up the stairs, her robe trailing behind her, and ran into the study.

"Harry, please, come quick!"

Harry turned around in his chair and looked at his wife. Her eyes were two wild blue pools, her hair falling over them in tangles.

"Heavens, Helen, what's going on?"

"You have to come quick! Oh, god, please! It's terrible! Jim is being taken!"

He looked at her now, her eyes reddening, clutching a handkerchief firmly with one hand. He jumped out of his chair, "I'm coming!" He ran after her, skimming down the stairs to the living room. He approached it and looked inside. She pointed a trembling finger at it and turned away.

"Look!"

Their darling little twelve year old boy, Jim, lay on the chair in front of the T.V., slowly transforming into a shapeless blob.

"Turn that thing off!" she screamed. Harry moved towards the television and reached out his hand. Standing there, his hand froze.

"Helen, my hand!"

All across the neighborhood, all across the town, all across the country, children were slowly transforming into shapeless irregular blobs in front of the flashing images of the television screens.

"We'll have to move him," he said. "I'll help you with my good hand."

Helen cautiously approached the growing monstrosity, now a sickly green bulge on the thick carpet, his eyes staring ahead lethargically and his jaw dropping to his chest. She touched the smooth, rubbery surface lightly with her cold fingers. The pulpy flesh opened, and her fingers sank in! She let out a horrified scream!

"Helen!"

A wide hole opened in the blob, and her arm went in. As Harry tried to grab his wife's side, the pulp contracted and swallowed her whole. Harry wet his pants and moved back. The creature turned his lethargic eyes towards Harry. He glided over the carpet, his pulpy flesh spilling over it in voluminous folds. Harry pressed against the wall. The creature smiled grotesquely. A scream, and the creature was alone! Satisfied with his meal, he returned to watch some more T.V.

David Jager
Seventh Grade - 1981

Assignment 16 – Short Stories

Written by Groups of Students

Usually kids who are the same age have many similar experiences, so it's easy for you to get together in a small group and organize to tell a story. This is a step by step method I've used for small group short story writing:

1. You form small groups with two to six students per group.

2. Each small group decides on a story to tell and a point of view.

3. The number of students in a group determines the number of main events and main characters in the story.

4. Each group member selects a particular event to write.

5. After all events have been chosen, each student makes a <u>detailed</u> outline of the action in his/her event, and also writes the <u>last</u> paragraph of that event.

6. The writer of the first event gives a copy of his last paragraph to the writer of the second event who gives a copy of his/her last paragraph to the writer of the third event, etc. The writer of the last event doesn't have to give a copy of his/her last paragraph to anyone because he/she finishes the story. When last paragraphs are passed from writer to writer in this fashion, all members of a group are in a position to begin writing their events simultaneously.

7. When completed, the stories are read to the class, each member of a group reading his/her own event. There are a few interesting surprises with characters, dialogue, details of plot, and settings because members don't have to share their writing with other members of the group while they're in process. This group approach to short story writing also provides an interesting study of writing styles.

8. If your group finishes early and you like your story well enough, you may wish to try <u>translating</u> it into a short play. Each group member writes his/her story event as a scene for a short play. When completed, the group does a reading of its play for the class. Reading story and play side by side allows for an interesting study of <u>what</u> happens when one form of writing is changed into another form.

Assignment 17 - Reasoning

I'll explain four approaches to the "reasoning process," and you practice with your own examples of each of them.

The first approach deals with <u>analogies</u>. An analogy shows <u>similarities</u> between things that are otherwise dissimilar. The heart is like a pump; the lungs are like a bellows. It's fun to try to prove analogies true or false. "A teenager is to a caterpillar as an adult is to a butterfly." True or false? Prove it in a well thought out five to six paragraph, 250-300 word composition.

<u>Inductive reasoning</u> is a second common approach to the reasoning process. One way of practicing it is to simply decide on a topic and then begin gathering information about the topic from every available source: people, newspapers, magazines, books, radio, television, the internet, etc. As you gather your <u>facts</u> and <u>opinions</u> from different sources, begin writing <u>single sentence statements</u> about the most important information. At weekly intervals, examine the specific <u>single sentence statements</u> you've made about your topic and combine that thinking in <u>single sentence generalizations</u>. Now select your best <u>generalization</u> as a <u>theme</u> and write a <u>short play</u> or <u>short story</u> which develops that idea. You'll be practicing <u>deductive reasoning</u> when you do this.

<u>Logic</u> is a third commonly practiced form of reasoning. Actually, when you write a good story, you are practicing a kind of logic, narrative logic, the kind that says one event must follow another in a sequence and be related in a cause-effect way to make sense. However, narrative

logic is just another form of logic. Another kind is syllogistic. Here's an example of it:

All students grow.
Conformity is an unconscious part of growing up.
Therefore, all students are unwitting conformists.

Try to write a well-balanced argument which shows two sides for the above reasoning.

The fourth and final kind of reasoning I'd like you to practice is your personal reaction to an <u>idea</u>. For this assignment, let the idea be "freedom." In your first paragraph, explain what "freedom" means to you. In your second, third, and fourth paragraphs, discuss your <u>theories</u> for making "freedom" really work in the family, at school, and among your friends. In the fifth and final paragraph sum up your thinking about "freedom."

"Caterpillar or Butterfly"

A teenager is to a caterpillar as an adult is to a butterfly.

On the surface, a teenager and caterpillar are very similar to one another. Each has a body which, while maturing, goes through homely, cute, and ugly stages. Oh, of course, they don't resemble each other physically (let's hope not!), but they go through the same period of awkward development which is very evident. So, we see their outside cover. More important, however, is what goes on inside these changing shells.

In the life of a teenager, the drastic change from childhood to adulthood is overbearing, and he strikes out at the world through rebellion, surliness, and with a chip on his shoulder. He does things without thought and often with much emotion. So, too, the caterpillars. They eat leaves and fruit instinctively, without thought or anything else. They harm crops unknowingly, just as teenagers hurt people unconsciously. They, too, have to change drastically from egg to butterfly and have to keep up with the physical change, mentally.

Finally, the big day comes when the caterpillar breaks out of its homely shell and emerges as a winged flower, just as the adult breaks out of his teenage experiences and is launched into society as a fellow human being. The butterfly does not harm anything, but flies about doing good, being beautiful, and generally setting a good example for the caterpillars. It is allowed to fly, to see the world, and, I guess, anything else that is saved for the privileged butterfly in his society.

The adult is very similar. An adult does not hurt anyone, he thinks of everyone else before himself, and he sets a brilliant example for his followers, (theoretically), of course. But the greatest similarity between the teenager and the caterpillar and the butterfly and the adult is the amount of responsibility put on them. This sense of responsibility marks the distinct change from caterpillar to butterfly and from teenager to adult. That's life!

Judy Davenport
Ninth Grade - 1967

Inductive Reasoning

"Survival"

Specific Statements:

1. When faced with survival, panic is often present, but it only makes survival more difficult.

2. Organization is very important when surviving.

3. Determination should become stronger as survival becomes more difficult.

4. A group often has a better chance of survival than an individual.

5. When surviving, class favoritism shouldn't be present.

6. Often, people will display entirely different personalities and become less civilized as the desperation for survival becomes greater.

Generalization:

Survival is often more difficult than it should be because of a lack of organization, determination, and combined ideas and experience.

Maureen Donnels
Seventh Grade - 1969

"Freedom"

Freedom is very important to me. I like being able to express my feelings on a certain subject when I want to. Freedom to me means being able to speak out and say what I feel and being able to go anywhere I want. That's what it means to me.

I think that people could make "freedom" work in their families if they all wanted to. Of course, there would have to be some limitations. I don't think a kid can just leave to go anywhere, anytime he wants! That's not being responsible. But keeping a kid inside all the time, and making him work, and not letting him have any free time is pretty rotten, too! I think that if a child finishes cleaning his room, or taking out the garbage, that he should be rewarded with some free time to do something he wants to do.

Let's say that a teenager leaves his room like a pig sty, the garbage overflowing, and pop bottles lying all around the house. I don't think that he should be rewarded with free time because he already spent that time fooling around instead of doing his chores. So, his time is spent, and he will have to pay the consequences. I also think that if a child does something extra like cleaning the living room or dusting off the furniture, he should be offered a little more free time.

I think there should be freedom at school, but not too much! I don't think kids should be allowed to cut classes. I also don't think the rules should be as strict at the Army. Usually, they aren't.

I think that there should be a lot of freedom between friends. I don't think that a person should hang around just one friend all the time. First of all, you usually get sick of each other after a while because you're around each other so much. And second of all, you don't get a chance to make new friends. I think that the more friends you have the richer you are. In some cases there should be a lot of freedom, and in other cases there should be a little freedom. But in all cases, freedom is important, very important!

Suzanne Dieter
Seventh Grade - 1981

Assignment 18 - Essays

An <u>essay</u> is your <u>personal response</u> to any topic. Sometimes essayists tell a short story to catch your attention before they wade into and develop their main idea. If you do this, try to begin with a story that is related to the main point you're trying to make. As you study the student-written essays, you'll notice that many different approaches to the topics are used, but all of the students are reacting personally to the topics with their thinking and feeling. After reading the examples, write essays on topics which hold interest or concern for you today.

"Growing Up"

"Teenagers! Teenagers! They're so rowdy and wild!" So many parents and adults have uttered these words in disgust and anger. They say this because of one act, one deed of a teenager they haven't so much as met or seen, but just read about.

They are being unusually unfair about the entire situation when they say that all teenagers are "a band of ruffians, foolishly allowed to run wild in the streets." They don't seem to realize how a reporter can slant a story or how many violent crimes adults commit every day, or that they, too, were once young adults seeking understanding.

That is the key word right there, <u>understanding</u>. As the situation stands now, many parents act like pompous so-and-so's who want only to dominate, but won't think for one instant that they are partially responsible, that they are one of the contributing factors to the behavior of their children. If parents would only give a try at understanding a teenager's problems and respecting their thoughts and ideas, things would be much happier all the way around.

I'm not saying that all parents are bad, or that all the blame be placed on the parents' shoulders. I'm simply saying that they should try to improve, just as the teenagers should. Many parents do not make the effort to understand. Some go all out for it and nearly baby their children to death. These situations with parents bending too far either way may be encountered anywhere, but both are harmful to the child.

If parents would only give understanding a try, to try and learn from their teenagers as well as teach them, delinquency and angered parents would slowly diminish.

Eleanor Henry
Seventh Grade - 1961

"Communication"

Fads come and go, sweeping the United States into a turbulent whirlpool of modernity. New ideas change clothing fashions, language patterns, musical expressions, and complete ways of life. The "in" thing is usually the thing a person does wanting to be accepted by his fellow man, and thus a cultural happening develops.

Present cultural experiences are the family way of life, the worshipping of a God, the segregation of races, and a blaming of bad things on the hippies and the communists.

A new fad may develop, a new cultural experience, since the world is forever changing. The cultural experience I would like to see occur is the acceptance of communicating, whether it is on a one-to-one basis or on a one to a whole country. If people were willing to communicate, most of the world's problems would dissolve. People would slow down their hectic pace, enabling them to listen to others express their thoughts. Free speech would bloom everywhere. Talks in parks, groups of people in the middle of nowhere, rapping, songs being sung with messages, people saying "I understand" -- all normal in a society where communication has arisen.

If the old people talked to the young, if the white people spoke to the black, if the intelligent spoke with the dumb, if the straight people spoke with the unruly, if the doves talked to the hawks -- and if all listened to each other and actually communicated, life would be simpler and fuller. People would greet perfect strangers with "hello" without feeling weird, wrong telephone numbers would not embarrass the two parties, flat car tires would not be a silent "wait and see what happens" deal. In general, the darkness of never being introduced to a person would grow lighter.

Talking is a human ability. In present-day America, it is better to be seen than heard. If a cultural adjustment did occur, people would laugh in public, elevator operators would talk about more than just the weather, disc jockeys would say more than just their stations' call letters, politicians would say more than, "Let me make this perfectly clear," and the lady at 767-111 would be alive instead of taped. Communication would spread across the globe and make forms of human expression transferable.

Everyone would listen, talk, read, write, sing, dance, paint, express how they feel, <u>COMMUNICATE!</u>

Carole Chudwick
Eighth Grade - 1970

"Violence on Earth"

The word "violence" is a household word. A day cannot pass without mention of it, whether it is covered in newspapers, on television, on radio, or its actual presence faces you. Total peace reigns nowhere on this planet. The lands are scarred by wars of the past, and new wounds open daily due to violence of the present.

Bombs explode in downtown areas; men with telescopic rifles shoot at people from perches far above; murders, robberies, and rapes take place in dark alleyways of big cities; riots tear apart campuses; and cities and wars thrive on violence of the present.

But who is to say what violence has a cause and purpose, and which does not? Whose decision is it to say that the battles of the Mekong Delta are anymore justified than the bombing of a Manhattan skyscraper and the day of the bomb scares that followed? Who has the knowledge and the authority to say that the firing of buckshot by police at youths in Berkeley is more legal than the supposed conspiracy done by the Chicago Seven?

No man can claim to be God, but some men take it upon themselves to set the standards by which all men must live. They condemn some violence, and then say that to take part in other violence is a person's patriotic duty. This is having your cake and eating it, too, and human lives mean more than that. Killing never solved anything. Its only reward is death to someone's loved one, its only sorrow the fact that the stupid, senseless murders will continue as long as man allows one kind and condemns another. People suffer due to both.

Violence is as old as man himself, and the longer we wait to stop it, the harder it will be. A sudden overnight change is impossible; a law proclaiming all violence a federal crime will do no good. What must change? The hearts of men. The want to harm other creatures must end, the sport of killing wild beasts must stop, the manufacturing of weapons world-wide must cease, the need for no police officers must come about - for what are policemen but reminders of the fact that violence does occur, and the toy guns that spark violence must become obsolete.

Man must desire a passive world before he can obtain one, and only if the things mentioned above come about will he have one.

The process is a slow one, I think, for man will have to adjust to the new conditions in his world. He will weigh heavily the past and the future, and his mind will be boggled by the confronting situation because man is basically a violent animal. His nature tells him to kill to survive, but if he kills, someone else dies. Death is the ultimate, the end. Do people want to die? Some must, I think. Those that have the crazy want to see blood and pain. Those that kill children as they leave a school bus. Those that massacre civilian women and children in Vietnam.

What will become of these people in a peaceful world? Their hearts cannot be changed because they believe in what they are doing. If they do believe in killing, what can the passive man do to them? There would be no way to reform their violent ways, and their execution would be the end of man's new life.

All that could be done to these violent people would be to send them to a new land where they could set up a new life that they believe in - a human jungle.

Violence must become a word of the past, or it will destroy every living thing in its path towards supposed good and justice.

Carole Chudwick
Eighth Grade - 1970

"Is Patriotism Dead"

What is it that brings tears to a citizen's eyes when the national anthem is sung? What makes chills run up and down one's spine at the sight of the Stars and Stripes against a clear blue sky? What is it that inspires great poets and writers to set down on paper the spirit of America? What creates the feeling of awe and pride in an American's heart when a mounted or military color guard passes by, and every head is bare? Could it be a dead cause? No! It is alive, very much alive, and that cause is <u>patriotism</u>!

Simply because American citizens are not dashing through the streets, waving flags and shouting at the tops of their voices, is no ground for the supposition that patriotism is dead.

Concern for the welfare of our nation is far from dead. Some people see the matter in that light because the World War I and the World War II prototypes of patriotism are undergoing a transformation. If a statue of patriotism, as it is, could be made, it would probably be a proud eagle bearing "Old Glory," perched on the shoulder of a saluting, bravely-smiling soldier who is singing "God Bless America." But now this statue is only a chunk of metal, having been reduced to such by friction, heat of anger, and possibly a bit of neglect. Nevertheless, the basic concept of patriotism is still there, as it will always be, no matter how much it is beat upon and attacked by radicalism. Who knows what form the statue will be given next by the chisels of the American people.

Perhaps when this statue is again complete, it will be partially unrecognizable to us. Right now, however, there seems to be something missing. Some element of emotion has disappeared. It may be that when the words "my country" are spoken by an American citizen, a full realization of the true meaning is lacking. After all, we <u>are</u> citizens of this nation, not simply inhabitants! But somehow there does not seem to be the same manner of pride and strength in the way the phrase is uttered.

In my opinion, the Vietnam confrontation is in large part responsible for this. During the two World Wars, the United States Armed Forces were protecting both our country and our ideals; whereas, in this Asian "policing action," it is questionable whether our country is on the offensive or defensive. I strongly suspect the former. These questions have been asked countless times by men and boys who have been inducted: "What cause am I fighting for? Why should I fight in a political war that hasn't ever been declared?"

Some of today's young people would answer this question with a simple, "You shouldn't." The younger generation, so magnified by today's social gap, appears to have quite a different opinion of patriotism than their older fellow Americans. They seem to feel that true patriotism consists of acting in the way that will benefit their country most. This can mean standing up and stating one's feelings as to what is right or wrong. Unfortunately, some thoughtless radicals have carried this concept to an extreme. Those people who burn the American flag and resort to violence are little more than spoiled children who are not capable of behaving in a civilized manner which would be fruitful for all concerned. In these individuals, patriotism is indeed dead, or possibly it never lived. Worst of all, these people have created a bad reputation for those young people who are conscientious in their protests.

Are the citizens, whose sincere concern about national affairs leads them to speak out, to be considered less patriotic than those who follow and concur with whatever pattern of existence their country offers? Again I say, "No." This difference of opinion is a reaction to the changing form of patriotism.

In conclusion, I can only say again that the fire of patriotism still burns, and that as long as there are sparks of life in American hearts, such a fire will never die. For it is these sparks which feed the flame, and the act of giving of one's self which provides the fuel. If we all do our part in tending the flame, when patriotism emerges from this present metamorphic stage, America, and each of us, will be better for it.

Sue Grant
Ninth Grade - 1970

"To All the Youth of America Who Want Change"

Did you know that we, the youth of America, have nothing about which to protest? That our world is not at all in very bad shape?

So what if 50,000 Americans and over one million Vietnamese have been killed in Vietnam, if we see our own black, yellow, and red brothers beaten in the streets and shoved into ghettos where rats and roaches crawl along with filthy heroin pushers among sad, sick, and cold children, if our so-called "law enforcers" kill anybody with whom they disagree and won't offer help to anybody dressed in a "hippie" style, if our air is so polluted with deadly gases that we will soon have to wear gas masks to breathe, if the threat of a nuclear war hangs over our heads at all times!

No, we need not protest. God made earth for man to destroy. He made blue skies to fill with deadly gases. He made men to kill one another. We are just trying to be impossible for the adults. Why not let them worry about this world. They were once our age. They have more experience.

Yet, did they ever have to face a future like ours? A future so sick there might as well not be one? When our future has come, they will be gone, and yet, they were the ones who formed our future. They sure made a bummer!

Why can't we form our own future? Then we may have a society that we want, a society where people love together, get together, have peace and enjoy life, where all are equal. Yet how can we get it? We've got to change, now!

Yes, we do have something about which to protest!

Dayna Green
Seventh Grade - 1970

"Utopia"

What would happen if the United States became a nation of loving people who respected one another? I think that if everyone loved and respected everyone else, we would have a much better country. All of our current problems relate to a lack of love. If a man were about to steal something, he would not because he would love the person from whom he was about to steal. There would be no wars! It would be like eternal peace in the United States. No hardships would exist. The pollution problem would solve itself. Everyone would love his neighbor, so no one would send wastes into the air that would eventually kill others.

Companies would go out of business. There would be no need for locks or policemen. However, policemen would all soon be working again because everyone would love them and feel sorry for them. Consequently, jobs would be offered, and there would be no unemployment.

Racial problems would be solved, and poverty would soon disappear. If everyone loved one another, they would care about their fellow human beings and try to help them. Buildings, brand new, with electricity, heat, beds, refrigerators, and running water would shoot up. Disease would soon be conquered. Everyone would get together and fight the bugs and run them down. Just enough would be here so there would be no chance for them to become extinct. Other animals would not be extinct either because everyone would cooperate in helping them.

A normal day in your life would go like this: You would wake up, get dressed, go out, greet your mother and tell her to go back to bed and catch up on her sleep. She might do just that. After your breakfast, you wash your dishes. Since you were already late, and your mother would realize this, she would offer to make your bed for you.

After climbing on the bus which had been waiting patiently for you, you'd be on your way to school. When getting off, your fellow students would always let you go first. You'd go through school normally. The only change would be that you would always do your homework for the teacher because you'd love her. After getting home, you'd play with your dear brothers and sisters who <u>never</u> bothered you. There would never be any arguments between anyone in your family. It would always be harmonious and happy.

Unfortunately, war might be continued. It might because everyone else in the world might not be loving, only the people in the United States. There is a possibility that we might be able to work out some agreement, but there would be no guarantee. We would be a very easy country with which to settle disputes, so other countries might try harder to negotiate with us.

There would be no crimes, no murders, no thefts, and people wouldn't bother anyone else. Everyone would be happy! If there was anyone sad, others would try to cheer him up.

I am wondering if this could actually come true. Some day, could such a world be established? Maybe, but only with everyone's cooperation, which is difficult to get.

Would it even be a fun world in which to live? Would there be any kind of challenge in a world where everyone loved everyone else? There might be, but everyone would act and be alike. No one would be different. It would be like everyone was one person. It is your decision to make because you have to live in your world, not someone else's.

Anne Rieman
Seventh Grade - 1970

"Friendship"

Friendship is a quality without which man cannot live peacefully. Man needs companionship. He needs love. He needs friendship. Without these he cannot live in harmony with his fellow man.

The main issue is attention. A man basks in attention, and without it he feels inferior. So, he strives to gain attention. Many times he becomes a trouble-maker. This gives him the attention he needs, but it makes him even more inferior, and the cycle continues. I, myself, do not find a friend in this type of person. Don't get me wrong; I'm not prejudiced, nor do I classify people. I socialize briefly with many, and if they do not suit my taste (qualities I appreciate), I go on to others. This may seem mechanical and too orderly, but it's not. In reality, I play it by ear. I don't really see it as a task.

This is the way I make friends: by happenstance. It works good, too. And I have many friends to prove it. I also find that once I find a friend, he stays my friend for a very long time. I credit this to many things. Mutual trust ranks number one. Without this a relationship splits wide open. You must be able to trust someone to relate to them. Many things you want to talk about or discuss should be held confidential because a friend is one in whom you can confide.

Another important trait in a relationship is respect, respect for the friend's emotions, opinions, and tastes. This is as important as trust.

There are other qualities concerning friendship, but, of course, it's up to you to rank them.

Doug Grow
Eighth Grade - 1973

"Love"

Love is the hardest emotion to describe. When parents are asked what it is, they normally say something like, "Well, it's when you like someone a lot." Of course, kids aren't usually satisfied with that explanation, so they ask how they'll know when they love someone. By now, the parents are totally baffled, so they say something like, "Don't worry, when you're in love, you'll know it."

And, amazingly enough, they're right!

There's an old saying that says, "Love is never having to say you're sorry." That's the <u>biggest</u> farce that has ever existed. Love is saying you're sorry. This shows you respect the other's feelings, which is very important in establishing a relationship. I, myself, greatly appreciate a meaningful relationship. To me, love is the highest stage of "like" you can get. It is the best feeling you can possibly have. It is the highest quality of life available to a human. It should be treated with the highest respect possible. I do this, and I find I get respect in return, and this pleases me very much.

Love is also loyalty. I find this trait especially strong in my pets. They're both poodles, and they're very loving. Many times they've run away, but something always seem to pull them back, and for this I'm grateful. This must prove that loyalty, along with companionship and many other qualities, traits, and emotions accompany the almighty <u>LOVE</u>!

In my life, I've made many wishes, but now, if I were to make one wish, I would wish that love would be contagious.

Doug Grow
Eighth Grade - 1973

"Plants"

Willamina is a huge piggy-back plant in our living room. One day she told me her life story: "When I was a little sprout, I was taken away from my mother and put into a pot all by myself. I was so lonely I almost wilted. But the lady that cared for me kept giving me just the right amount of water and put me on a windowsill. There I watched the sun coming up over the hills every day. I loved the morning sun, and when it touched my leaves, it made me forget how lonely I was. Well, I grew and grew, and the next thing I knew I had a little plant all of my own."

Plants can add color to our lives. They can be used for decorating houses and yards. Caring for plants can make us feel closer to the outdoors. Plants can be used to spruce up our houses, and they add a healthy atmosphere to our homes. They make us more aware of other living things and let us breathe a little easier.

No house can breathe without plants for decoration. Putting plants in a kitchen would make it seem more cheerful and spacious. Hanging plants make a house seem more airy. Plants can be used outside for a border near a sidewalk or to enhance a deck or patio. For decorating, plants are a must.

Caring for the plants which decorate our homes puts us in touch with life. Watching our plants grow gives us more understanding of them. We also learn to appreciate things like forests and parks more when we understand the plants in them. Nature can be brought into our hearts and minds more when we know about plants.

Nature in our houses creates a healthy environment. Plants breathe out oxygen and breathe in carbon dioxide. We do just the opposite. Besides being medically healthful, plants are nice, too, when you're sick and in bed. If we stay around plants a lot, we also might be healthier.

Healthy people use plants in many different ways. Plants enrich our life styles. We should be grateful we have them.

Stephanie Ruehman
Seventh Grade - 1976

"Books"

This is a discussion of six different books based on teenagers and some of the problems with which they are faced.

The books, <u>Durango Street</u> and <u>Rumbelfish</u>, deal with young kids about twelve to nineteen, growing up, going into gangs. In <u>Durango Street</u> it's easy to enter a gang because everyone's in one, and they're always after you if you aren't. <u>Durango Street</u> takes place in a Black ghetto. <u>Rumbelfish</u> is another book about gangs. They end up heavy on drugs and are usually robbing and getting into fights.

Some other drug problems are in the books <u>Go Ask Alice</u> and <u>Sarah T. Go Ask Alice</u> is a true diary about an average girl, not on drugs or anything until she's invited to a party and someone drugs her drink. After that she tries drugs once again and then again and again, finally getting addicted. She ends up dying of an overdose, but no one knows if she did it herself or if someone drugged her again because before she dies, she was on the verge of getting off drugs. <u>Sarah T.</u> is another book about drugs, but it's alcohol which has basically the same effect. Sarah T. was forced to turn into an alcoholic because her mom was always on her back, and she needed something to make her feel good. Although she was a heavy alcoholic, she was one of the few lucky ones that survived. She ended up going to a hospital and getting help. These books show you how you can turn out if you choose to live this way. Sarah T. turned out O.K, but she still wasted about two years of her life.

The book, <u>Dawn</u>, is about this girl, Dawn, whose mother is an alcoholic. Dawn can't stand watching her mother throw away her life any more, so she decides to run away. She goes to a big city and meets a guy. He lets her stay with him. She has to find some sort of job just so she can eat. She is forced to turn to the streets. Another book dealing with this type of thing is <u>Little Ladies of the Night</u>. It's about a lady who's jealous of her daughter because her husband is always spending time with the daughter. Actually, it's about the girl because she can't stand the jealousy anymore and decides to run away. This one guy meets her at the bus and decides to please her by buying her rich clothes and giving her a place to live. One day he says she owes him something. So, he forces her to turn to the streets. She tries to call her dad, but her mother answers the phone and says to stay where she is because she and her husband are getting along just fine. The daughter ends up slitting her wrists and dying.

There are many teenagers with more problems, but this gives you an idea of some of them. It looks like it's not always the kids' or the parents' fault. It's a very rough world, and I only hope I don't end up like one of these people. I'll try my hardest not to.

Lisa Elgin
Ninth Grade - 1978

"My Future"

I should begin to plan my future because it will be very important later in life. To start with, I should figure out the general area in which I wish to work. Secondly, I should plan my upcoming choice of classes around this selection. In these classes I should give my all and get the best grades I can. Then I should get experience in the field of my interest and go on to college. Then my plan will be completed by obtaining that job I prepared for over the past years.

Picking the general area in which I'll be working in the future is pretty hard. There are numerous tests that are taken in the junior high years that show some of my general interests. Even then, if I wish, I can go into a totally different field. I should talk to people in these job areas in which I am interested. All I can really do is read, ask, and experience different ones, and I will probably find a general interest.

After recognizing the general field, I should begin to plan my classes and time around them. I should take classes which are recommended for that category of jobs and prepare for them. While taking these classes, I should pay attention to the specializations of jobs within this interest area. Then I should pretty much find out what I want to do.

After high school I should either get work experience in my job or go on to college for further preparation, or both. A lot of high-paying jobs call for college classes and different degrees. Before I go to college and take these special classes, I should be sure that I'm going into that field. College costs a lot of money, so I don't want to go for something I'll only be doing for a few years.

After all my preparation, it's time to go out and find that job with my credentials. Sometimes the school you previously have graduated from can give you job openings. I'll probably tend to find that the people with the highest credentials will be placed above others. I have then succeeded in my plan. From then on I'll just have to cope with one problem, staying happy in that job.

In conclusion, I think that planning for my future is very important. I should be thinking about what field I'd like to be going into right now. Through high school I'll have to stay on the books a lot and keep up my grades in hopes of getting a scholarship. I'll work hard in college and get that job I worked for, then hope it was the right one for me.

Linda Foy
Ninth Grade - 1978

"Everyone A Winner"

Attending the Special Olympics was a very exciting experience for many people on Saturday, May 13, 1978. It was especially rewarding for me. Bailey Field was the location of this interesting event. All kinds of participants came from all over Sonoma County. I am especially hoping that after all those people who attended spread the word, that both mentally and physically handicapped people will be as readily accepted as any other normal American person.

Going to the Special Olympics was a great and rewarding experience for me. Just being there gave me a tingle in my heart. I think it rewarded me with an experience of helping special kinds of people which is my main goal in life. I left with a feeling of satisfaction and happiness.

The meet was held at Bailey Field in Santa Rosa, California. I thought that was an ideal place for the event. There were grandstands for many spectators and for the participants to sit during the various events. Also, the huge oak trees on the grassy middle section of the track provided a good amount of shade. The weather was warm, but that didn't stop the thousands of spectators who came to this fantastic event.

Many different groups came and participated in the Special Olympics. Some groups were from Sonoma State Hospital, Creative Living Center, and Steele Lane School, and participants ranged in age from six years on up. Their handicaps were varied, too. Mentally retarded, physically handicapped, and blind children all participated. The physically handicapped entered field events such as the softball throw, and the mentally retarded competed in running races. There was a wheelchair race, a blind person's race, and a walk-a-later race. Altogether there were 800 participants, 500 from Sonoma State Hospital alone.

To me, going to the Special Olympics was one of the most beautiful experiences I have ever encountered. I feel that after attending the Special Olympics, a lot of people will have a better understanding of these special people. I would like to see a little more respect and care for physically and mentally handicapped people. I know I care and have respect for them. These special human beings are some of the sweetest people I have ever met. When a mentally retarded boy, whom you've never met before, reaches out his severely deformed arm and hand, talks to you, and before leaving gives you a kiss on the cheek and tells you he loves you . . . well, I think that is all I have to say. I know this day brought tears to my eyes, and maybe some day an experience as beautiful as the one I had will bring tears to your eyes, too.

Denise Hirsh
Ninth Grade - 1978

"Life's Value"

In the beginning of October we were doing gymnastics in P.E. I was attempting to do a handstand when I kicked up too hard. I went up and all the way over, landing flat on my back. I lay on the mat for a minute because I felt a slight pain in my back, but then I got up and went through a normal day with no pain. The next day, I felt pain in my back, but I didn't think it was anything serious.

About two weeks passed with slight pain until one morning I got out of bed and couldn't stand up straight. My parents thought I should go to a chiropractor, so I did. After about two weeks of his treatment, he admitted that my back wasn't responding as he had expected.

Then I went to our family doctor. He suggested that I go to an orthopedic surgeon, a specialist who deals with back problems. I was beginning to wonder if I would have to walk crooked for the rest of my life. Anyway, I ended up in the hospital.

In the hospital I had to take a test called a myelogram which showed all the nerves, blood vessels, and soft tissues surrounding the vertebra. To take the myelogram, the doctor had to inject a dye into my spinal column. The only problem, the doctor said, was if I were to be allergic to the dye. Another problem was if he didn't get all the dye out, it would cause problems later. The test showed I had a herniated disc which was pressing on the nerves to my legs, cutting off the blood supply to the nerves of my left leg and causing me to lose control of my left foot.

I was going to have an operation. During the operation there would be a chance of losing most of my leg muscles or that I wouldn't walk again! There was also a possibility that the operation wouldn't do any good.

Lately, I've learned to value my life, good health, and happiness more than ever before. Most young people forget about the importance of good health. Not me! Already because of my back I'm limited in certain things. Now, I realize how important it is to have good health. I also value happiness because if I'm not happy, I can't enjoy all the good things in life.

I also value my life because of my family. When I was in the hospital, my family came and visited me every day and helped pass the time with me. My family also gives me love, security, advice, happiness, care, ideas, etc.

Another reason I value my life is because of friends. My friends and I do a lot of things together like fishing, square dancing, homework, etc. My friends also give me help, people with whom I can talk, keep company, exchange ideas, and support.

I value my life for the freedom and the ability I have to develop new interests like fishing, model building, and repairing small engines.

This back problem has made me starkly aware of the importance of my health, happiness, family, friends, and new interests and how they all contribute to my desire to live.

Dean Mori
Ninth Grade - 1979

110

"Being Handicapped"

Being handicapped can be very difficult. For most handicapped people it is hard to play sports. Transportation can be very difficult and expensive. It's also hard to make friends, as well as get your shopping done. Handicapped people, especially ones in wheelchairs, find it very hard to get through doors. All these things add up and can be extremely frustrating.

It's hard for handicapped people to do a lot of sports. If you're deaf, you couldn't hear a whistle blown by a referee or the coach yelling. If you were in a wheelchair and couldn't run, there might be some sports you could do like basketball, swimming, horseback-riding, and bowling with special ramps, but they'd all present special problems and be difficult to perform.

Besides sports, another hard thing for the handicapped is transportation. Some wheelchair people have special cars with wheelchair lifts that lift them up to the car and then fold up. Then they roll up to the front, have the seat removed, and with hand controls drive the car. When they finally get to their destination, it's often hard to get through the doors. A lot of old buildings have doorways that are too small for wheelchairs, but now it is a state law that any new buildings or remodeled buildings must have enlarged doorways in the bathrooms and offices.

Some handicapped people have to worry about shopping if they live alone. There could be stairs in front of a store, or the doorway might be too small. Pushing a cart is practically impossible if you're in a wheelchair, and then if you want something on a top shelf, how are you going to get it?

Many handicapped people have very few friends besides their families, and when some people see handicapped people, they're afraid of befriending them because they're different.

When you think about it, handicapped people work very hard just to get through one day. They deserve a lot of credit for the things they do. Maybe someday you'll meet a handicapped person and think a little differently about him because of what I've said.

John Asti
Eighth Grade- 1981

"Family Love"

We had soccer tryouts last week. I thought I had done exceptionally well, and made it. A week after tryouts, the coach, Mr. Maroni, called and said I didn't make the team. I put the receiver down and ran to my room. I was crying and feeling sorry for myself. I cried so much that I didn't realize two hours had passed. Before I knew it, it was dinnertime.

My dad called me down for dinner. I refused to eat at that moment because I felt so bad. My dad walked into my room and said, "Why don't you want to eat?" I was trying to keep from crying, but by accident a tear fell from my eye. My dad knew something was wrong, and he asked me if I wanted to talk about it. I said, "Yes," and then told him what happened. I felt better right away because my dad gave me lots of love. He explained to me that I could try out next year, and he said that just because I didn't make it didn't mean I was a horrible player, which I thought I was.

I felt a lot better and decided that I would eat. At the dinner table we talked about what fun we would have going down the water slides as a family during the weekend.

I value the love of my family. When I'm down and upset, my parents will come up to me and make me feel better. They understand me, and I understand them. You could say we communicate very well. Like sometimes when I don't make the soccer team, get an "A" in World Geography, or someone hates me, they'll always come up to me and discuss the problem. They'll tell me how I should approach it and how I should handle it.

We share out love, ideas, laughter, fun, and lots more. We do lots of fun things together like sail, travel places, go on picnics, and many other things that involve family activity.

My family gives me support when I need it. When I'm nervous or scared, they'll tell me not to worry and that I'll be fine. Even though they may not say much, it's enough to make butterflies disappear. What I'm trying to say is that my family gives me love, warmth, happiness, etc.

My mom once said that I'd make many friends and have good relationships with them, and she was right, but to me they're just not the same as family.

Steve Bell
Seventh Grade - 1981

"Dad"

One afternoon my father came to visit us. He and I went out to lunch and had a great time.

That night while I was waiting for my dad to come in and kiss me goodnight, I started thinking about what it would be like to live with him or stay with him for awhile. When he came in, we started talking, and then I asked him if I could go back to his house with him. He went into the living room to discuss it with my mom. When he came back, he said I could go. It didn't take me long to pack my clothes. I said good-bye to my mom, and we left.

I stayed with my dad for five days. I had a lot of fun. We talked a lot about problems I was facing at school and about him and my mom. We also played chess (I only beat him once), ate salad, and just goofed around.

I loved staying with my dad, and I hope I can do it again some day.

I value many things in life, but the one thing I value the most is my father. I value my father for many reasons. I value him because he is very kind and understanding and because he always talks with me when I have problems or when I am troubled or confused. He helps me with my homework when I'm stuck, and he gives me good advice.

Another reason why I value my father is because I don't see him very often, and he doesn't live with us.

I love both of my parents very much, but I have a very special love for my father. I know that my mother and father will never remarry, but they still love each other.

I will always value my father wherever he is or whatever he does.

Cindy Polly
Seventh Grade - 1981

Essay Structure Sample

Jogging is a rewarding activity.
shape
endurance
mental

people
<u>Running</u> is a sport that really <u>pays</u> off.

Jogging is a rewarding activity. It helps a person keep in shape. Also, one's endurance is enhanced by jogging. Some joggers even claim they're better off mentally after this kind of exercise. And, of course, jogging increases one's chance of meeting new people. Running by oneself or with others is an active sport which pays off in different ways.

One way it pays off is by helping a person keep fit. Flab gradually melts away, and happy muscles once again become finely tuned and toned. That BIG MUSCLE, the HEART, begins increasingly circulating life-giving blood to all parts of the body. And our bellows-like lungs gradually increase their capacity to inhale air and thus make an increased oxygen supply available for the body's use. Keeping in shape prepares the body for other activities, too.

Some of these other activities require a great amount of endurance which jogging helps build. Cross-country running, swimming, or simply riding a bicycle a long way to school and back home use up a lot of energy. Do you think a person could do any of these or go out and run around the track four or five times without endurance? No way! Very early in the game the jogger learns to persevere, and as new goals are set, determination becomes a necessity. A kind of endurance is developed which becomes a part of both the body and the mind while jogging, especially the mind because the mind wills the body to do its bidding once the body is in shape.

Not only does the mind learn to endure and become strengthened while jogging, but it also becomes energized. The senses bring peaceful sights and sounds of Mother Nature to the brain which finds them relaxing. The stresses of one's daily schoolwork are forgotten for awhile, and both muscle and brain are allowed to ripple and relax. This rested mental state gives a person a chance to review what's happened and to think about what's going to happen. It gives a person a chance to be by him or herself and to simply think about life. Jogging is good therapy.

If the therapy one needs precludes being alone, there are always plenty of friends out there nowadays with whom to run, and they're usually the friendly people who smile a lot and like to talk. And when you get tired, many of them will even accommodate you by just walking and talking. Joggers seem to be nice people to meet. It's understandable. They respect themselves, and they'll more than likely respect and like you, too. So, get out there and start jogging and meeting some new friends.

If you want to hit the JACKPOT of physical and mental health, don't gamble. Face reality and start doing something with your life, today! Start jogging! You'll like it! You'll like what it does for you! It's an insurance policy with great dividends.

Essay Exercise

Next, try writing a 500-1,000 word essay which contains an introductory paragraph, like the essay above, only three middle paragraphs this time, and a concluding paragraph. In the sample essay, did you notice the "transitions" I used to move from the last sentence of a paragraph to the first sentence of the paragraph following it? Make this essay about a topic with which you are familiar, you. The main idea of your essay will be the sentence I've typed below. Use it as the first sentence of your introductory paragraph.

_____, _____, and _____ are the three most important qualities I will need to develop in order to lead a happy and successful life.

Assignment 19 - One Theme - Four Genre

An idea can be expressed in many different forms of writing. In the student examples which follow, a single idea or theme was written as a short play, short story, essay, and poem. The challenge is to control both <u>form</u> and <u>content</u> so you can consistently develop one theme in four different genre. If you can do this, you will also be learning that some modes of writing provide better vehicles for certain of your ideas than others. Select an idea or theme that is important to you and translate it into a short play, a short story, an essay, and a poem.

<u>Short Play - Fictional Group Experience One Theme - 4 Genre</u>

"A Dignified Winner"

Characters:
Julie Stevenson: 15 year old Olympic hopeful
Gail Pruitt: friend of Julie, also an Olympic hopeful
Mr. Elling: Julie's coach
Ella: Julie's mom
Mary: Julie's sister
Narrator
Announcer

Scene I.

Narrator: There are only two days before the gymnastics tryouts for the

U.S. Olympic Team. Tension is rising at the Stevenson house. (Fade in on Julie and her mom eating breakfast)

Ella: You're up early, Julie. Going down to the gym?

Julie: I have to work out. I don't want to go down to L.A. and forget my routine.

Ella: You look tired. Maybe you should skip a little this morning. You know that routine. You should rest awhile.

Julie: No, Mom. I'll be home early.

Mary: (Walks in and sees her mom's look of concern) What's wrong?

Ella: I'm just worried about Julie. She's been working herself too hard. All that pressure isn't good for her.

Mary: Don't worry, Mom. Julie can take care of herself. I'm going down to get the airplane tickets. Is Julie packed?

Ella: I don't think so. She's been spending all her time down at the gym.

Mary: When she gets home, tell her to get moving. We've got a plane to catch at 3:00!

Ella: She'll be ready on time.

Scene II.

(Cut to gym. Julie is doing her routine. Gail walks in.)

Gail: That was terrific, Julie!

Julie: I've got a lot of improving to do.

Gail: No, you're good! Have you packed your bags for L.A.?

Julie: No, Not yet.

Gail: I've been packed for a week! I still can't believe I qualified out of all those girls. It's going to be so much fun! Just think, next summer when I'm at home watching the Olympics , I can tell everyone that I know those girls.

Julie: It sounds like you're not even going to try!

Gail: I'll try, but I won't make it. Did you know there are thirty girls competing for the six places that make up the team? There's no way I'll be on it.

(Gail sees Julie's coach walking into the gym.)

Bye, Julie! I've got to go.

Mr. Elling: (walks over to Julie) Hi, Julie! Let's work on the beam. Maybe we can solve some of those problems you've been having. Start out slow and easy; get your timing together.

Narrator: Julie does her routine over and over, each time pushing for perfection.

Mr. Elling: Look, Julie, I know you're concentrating, you know you're concentrating, but the judges don't have to know. Do it once more and smile. Pretend the audience is out there. (He points to the other side of the gym.) You're in the spotlight, and the judges are watching every move you make.

Narrator: Julie is seeing everything. She's competing against the other girls, and she's doing her best. In her daze she is doing her routine perfectly. She doesn't make one mistake. When it's all over, she looks up and Mr. Eller is coming towards her, smiling.

Mr. Elling: That was sensational! Do it like that in competition! That's enough for today. I'll see you tomorrow morning at the tryouts. Get lots of sleep tonight and don't think about tomorrow.

Scene III.

Narrator: The first day of competition is over. Julie is two points out of first place after doing the vault and uneven parallel bars. Gail is holding a shaky eighth place. The second day of competition has Julie in first place after doing her floor routine. Gail has moved up to seventh, but only three points above eighth. The third day of competition Julie did her beam routine just like she had in practice. Gail is still in seventh place. It's the final day of competition.

Gail: Oh, Julie, I knew you'd come in first! You're so good! It's so exciting knowing the number one Olympic team star! I'm in seventh place. I really can't believe it and don't expect to stay there. I'll never be able to do all four routines today the way I did them the first time.

Julie: You'll do fine! Don't worry! Good luck! They're calling the lineup now. You'll do all right.

(The gym is darkened and sounds of cheering crowd are heard.)

Announcer: The final points for Gail Pruitt are: 5.8, 5.7, 5.3, 5.6, 5.5, 5.2, 5.6. This means that Miss Pruitt holds on to seventh place. Our next competitor is Lynn Segueira, currently holding third place.

(Crowd cheers. Cheering fades as Gail opens door to dressing room)

Julie: Congratulations! You did a good job out there.

Gail: I never thought I'd be in seventh place!

Announcer: Our final competitor is Julie Stevenson.

Gail: Go out there and hold first!

(Julie's already done two of her four routines. The spotlight is on Julie, standing on the beam for a second. Spot off.)

Announcer: That was a terrific forward flip! Now she's going for a round-off ending up in a split. Beautiful! Oh, no! She's fallen off the beam! This could cost her some points.

Mr. Elling: She's hurt! Get a doctor out there!

Announcer: Julie Stevenson who was in first place coming into the finals has fallen off the beam. She can't put any weight on her foot. It looks like it's her ankle. They're taking her off the platform now. There will be a delay in announcing the team standings. If Julie can't continue, that will move everyone up one place in the standings.

Mr. Elling: Put her in the dressing room.

Doctor: Let me take a look at that ankle.

Julie: Let me finish competing. It doesn't hurt.

Doctor: The ankle's broken.

Mr. Elling: You can't compete with a broken ankle!

Julie: It doesn't hurt! You can tape it up and after competition put it in a cast!

Mr. Elling: If you finish competing, you'll never be able to compete again!

Mary: Julie, if you continue, you might injure the ankle permanently! There's no sense taking that chance! You can try again in four years.

Julie: (sigh) All right.

Doctor: Send a runner out to the judges.

Mr. Elling: I'll go.

Announcer: We've just received word that Julie Stevenson has a broken ankle and will not finish competing. (Pause) This means that Gail Pruitt will be included in the Olympic team.

(The spotlight shines on Julie and Gail.)

Narrator: As Gail is walking towards the dressing room, Julie is coming out on her crutches.

Gail: (Hesitates) How's your ankle?

Julie: It'll probably be O.K. in a few weeks!

Gail: I'm really sorry, Julie. You're the one who deserves to be on the team not me.

Julie: Don't underrate yourself, Gail. You're a good competitor. I know you'll do well in the Olympics.

(Julie turns and walks away on her crutches. Gail is left in the spotlight, watching Julie leave. Then she turns her face directly into the spotlight. A few tears well down her cheeks.)

Voice: Hurry, Gail! You have to go to the winner's platform!

(Spotlight off)

Stephanie Ruehmann
Seventh Grade - 1976

Short Story - Fictional Family Experience One Theme - 4 Genre

"You Can Do It"

As the sun peeked over the hills, Bobby was just getting up. The breeze puffing at his curtains and the deep blue sky reminded him of yesterday morning when he got his bicycle.

Today was Saturday, so he hurriedly got dressed and went downstairs. His mom was fixing breakfast, and his dad was outside. As soon as he finished breakfast, Bobby ran outside to his dad. This was the second sunny day this week, and Bobby wanted to learn to ride his bike. He and his dad pulled the bike out of the garage, and Bobby got on it. Then they started down the sidewalk with Bobby's dad holding onto the back of the bike to keep it steady. Bobby was having a blast because his dad was doing all the work by running alongside the bike and pushing it. After five blocks with Bobby cruising down the sidewalk and his dad puffing behind, his dad called a halt to the expedition and headed for home. On the way back, Bobby's dad let go of him, and down Bobby went. He got up, scared and shaken. His dad had a hard time getting him back on the bike, but he finally succeeded.

When they got back home, it was time for some lemonade and a long rest in the shade, then back to the bike. The usually long afternoon became even longer to Bobby's dad. It wasn't easy pushing that bike. After Bobby's dad thought Bobby had the hang of keeping his balance, he let go, only to find that every time he let go of Bobby, the bike would wobble or fall.

Early afternoon with its hot sun found Bobby a very dejected and put-down boy and his father a very tired and worn out man. Every time Bobby fell off his bike, he got more discouraged, so when he hit a big rock on the sidewalk, he decided to give up. He'd had enough of this bike business. If it took that

121

much work to ride a bicycle, then he just wasn't going to learn. So Bobby picked up his bike and walked it home. He put it in the garage and walked slowly up the steps of his house. Going into the family room, he turned on the T.V. and plopped himself down. Then he picked up a bag of potato chips and started munching away his disappointment in himself.

In the meantime, Bobby's dad was thinking and knew Bobby could ride that bike if he wasn't scared of falling down. He also knew Bobby was very possessive. So, he quietly got the bicycle out of the garage and took it into the street. Bobby's dad then got on that little bicycle and began riding it in circles. Every time he brought his knees up, he rammed them into his chest. He had problems steering, too, because there wasn't enough room for his arms, and he kept sliding off the seat because it wasn't big enough. Despite these inconveniences he was going to ride that bike until Bobby came out there, which luckily wasn't that long.

Bobby was sitting next to the big window that looked out onto the street. Because of the noise his friends were making, he looked outside. At seeing his dad on his bike, he ran out to the street and yelled, "Daddy, you're riding my bike!"

His dad called back, "I'm not getting off until you come over here and tell me that you can ride a bike and that you'll prove it to me."

Enraged, Bobby said, "I can ride a bike!"

Before he knew it, he was on the bike, and his dad gave him a big push. He didn't know what to do. Then, remembering what his dad told him, he sat up straight and pedaled with all his might. He didn't realize how far he had ridden until his dad called out, "See! I told you it was easy!"

It was! Then Bobby realized he was riding a bicycle all by himself! A smile spread across his face. Beaming, he rode his bike up and down the street.

It was a proud but tired boy who later rode his bicycle into the garage for the night.

Stephanie Ruehmann
Seventh Grade - 1976

Essay One Theme 4 Genre

"You're A Winner"

Everyone is a winner. You have a talent. Talent is nourished by practice which grows success. With success comes self-pride. Confidence in your ability allows future successes. Winning is self-success.

Talent plays a large role in your success. Your talent might lie in a musical or dramatic field. Another talent is home skills such as working with wood, cooking, sewing, macrame', and decorating. Perhaps your talent is understanding and organizing people. Talent is the seed of success.

The seed sprouts into success through practice. If you are talented at playing an instrument, you must practice before you become good at it. If you have talent in baseball and you never practice, your natural skill will never develop. It will remain hidden to other people and yourself. Practice is the sunlight that causes talent to sprout into success.

The sunlight of self-pride glows upon you with success. If you succeed at something, you become proud of it. Pride in yourself creates a more complete person. You have to believe in yourself and have pride in yourself to be comfortable around other people. Pride glows through you, and other people will recognize it and accept it.

Accepting yourself comes with self-confidence. If you succeed at something, you have confidence in yourself. Other people will notice this confidence and admire it, but if you let too much confidence go to your head, watch out! No one likes a bragger. The right amount of confidence in yourself helps you along the path of winning at life.

Everyone travels down the path of winning. No one is a loser. Talent helped by a lot of practice will help you succeed. Self-pride and self-confidence will lead you to more success. Winning isn't hard, but you must work towards it.

Stephanie Ruehmann
Seventh Grade - 1976

Free Verse One theme - 4 Genre

"What Is Winning"

Winning is losing when you want to;
Winning is a breath of fresh air;
Winning is an "A" on your report card;
Winning is a new friend.

Winning is pretending you want to but don't;
Winning is finding yourself;
Winning is trying something new;
Winning is smiling through your tears.

Winning is finding someone who cares
And telling him how you feel;
Winning is sharing your ideas
And not being laughed at;
Winning is looking ahead and hoping.

Winning is walking with your head held high;
Winning is noticing the sun and sky;
Winning is everything I have mentioned, plus more.
Winning is doing what you believe is right,
No matter what other people think.

Stephanie Ruehmann
Seventh Grade - 1976

Assignment 20 - Autobiographical Poem

Write one verse of poetry for each year of your life. Idea, feeling, brevity, vivid language which creates sights, sounds, smells, touches, and tastes, and rhythm are all part of poetry. Rhyme isn't necessary, but it makes poetry fun to read.

Before you begin this assignment, discuss your early life with your family so you can learn what you were like and what important experiences you had when you were a little kid.

I struggle to reach out,
To say, "God, I see you!"
To believe.
I struggle to say,
"I am!" "I exist!"
I live in all certainty.
I struggle with tenacity,
Alone.

When I was one year old,
The world was very small,
Hardly a world at all,
But it was mine.

When I was two years old,
My rival came.
It had no name,

But I ruled no more.

When I was three years old,
The world was many things.
The ice cream man's ring.
I grew that year.

When I was four years old,
I went to nursery school.
I learned the meaning of rule.
The world was gray.

When I was five years old,
They placed me on a bus.
I didn't fuss,
Resigned to my fate.

When I was six years old,
School was fun.
Easy work, easily done.
The establishment laughed!

When I was seven years old,
My teacher didn't believe I'd
Written what I'd wrote.
I had to get a note.
I hated that woman!

When I was eight years old,
Math reared its ugly head.
I cried over problems in bed.
The world lost its lace.

When I was nine years old,
Competition was very strong.
I didn't last very long.
Alas, my innocence.

When I was ten years old,
Wrong was wrong, right was right.
Boys came into sight.
My future lay before me.

When I was eleven years old,
I fought to stay on top.
I matured. I couldn't take a flop.
Junior high had me scared.

When I was twelve years old,
No one said hello.
The halls were Big, and Oh,
I was alone!

Now I'm thirteen,
Calloused and aware.
I'll no longer take a dare.
I'm still alone.
The world is far too Big,
And I'm far too small.
I really don't belong,
At all.

Kim Haylock
Eighth Grade - 1970

At one I spoke my very first words.
I lay in my playpen and watched the toy birds.

I walked and ran when I was two.
I got some teeth and started to chew.

At three I learned to ride a trike.
I also met a friend named Mike.

I learned to swim at the age of four,
And I decided to ride my trike to the store.

I went to school when I was five
And waited for Santa Claus to arrive.

I lost some teeth when I was six.
We played cowboys just for kicks.

I went to Disneyland when I was seven.
It was really -- it felt like heaven.

I played Little League when I was eight.
I was growing, so I put on some weight.

We traveled to Texas when I was nine.
We saw the Grand Canyon, and it was fine.

Once more we went to Disneyland when I was ten.
It felt good to see it again.

When I was eleven, I was in sixth grade.
I didn't want to go to seventh -- I was afraid.

Well, now I'm twelve, alive and free.
And every single night I thank God that I'm me!

Tom Juarez
Seventh Grade - 1977

At one is rather hazy.
I'm sure I drove my poor mom crazy.
With all my whimpering complaint,
They quickly realized I was no saint.

But dear Dad 'n Mom taking this to heart,
Got me off to such a successful start
That by the age of two
It wasn't their loss
To have taught little Sharsie just who was boss.
Then all of a sudden an intruder came.
But dear sweet Mommy was not to blame.
The love she has knows no bounds.
There was more than enough to go around!

Three I finally got some hair
Which for me was something very rare.
I liked to color, to eat, and to play
And was nick-named Butterball to my dismay!
Of playmates for me there were many.
Dad and Mom gave them names: Evey, Lorr, Jul, and Jenny.

In my fourth year of life occurred something traumatic.
I broke my collarbone while being acrobatic!

Now for a four year old it was something quite tragic,
But with God and the doctors it healed like magic!
Came a time when Mom and Dad went "away"
And I was sent to Grandma's to stay.
It was called a "vacation," a "trip," a "rest."
When they returned with presents, I thought it the "best."

At five I was shy and going to school.
I loved my teacher and obeyed the rules.
I liked friends, rainy days, and dresses with lace,
But from the silly boys and their kisses, I found I must race.
That was also the year over the state we did roam,
Driven by Dad in our own motor home!

Six to school I was sent,
To learn about God and what it all meant.
The following year, when I turned seven,
St. Eugene's was my school, and they taught about heaven
And how we and the world began,
Because of the love of one wonderful man!

My eighth year was filled with other third graders,
Until the time for a new member came one year later!
We named him Roger Allen, and there never could be
A sweeter or cuter little baby than he.
That poor little guy, how did he fare?
Instead of one mother, he had six to care.

Wow! Moving into the two digit age was great!
I was getting older. Did that mean dates?
Not quite, Mom informs me, a few years to go.
Then I change schools -- Is there anyone I know?

Surprise! Can you guess? It's another addition.
I'm wondering - #8 - Is it becoming tradition?

Twelve is a blast! Life is ever so easy.
There are guys, camps, and parties - Oh! So breezy!
But soon the fun stops, and the fear sinks in,
For we hear of the horrors from our next of kin
About the big junior high and what goes on there,
About the ninth graders who'll send us quivering with a stare.

But look! Here I am starting school just the same,
It's new; it's exciting! I'm glad I came.
There are schedules, and lockers with combos so hard!
And even a few couples kissing out in the yard!
Moving on into eighth, how could I be so naive?
The work, the rules, the treatment -- it's hard to believe!
Things slow down - they seem to have stalled.

Hooray! I'm finally here.
I'm fifteen and this is my year!
What fun, what parties, what dances.
We'll run risks and take some chances!
But alas!
Life at fifteen is still rather hazy.
I'm sure it's these finals that are driving me crazy!
I'm young and I shan't be tied down,
I'll give it my best shot, and then I'll tour the town!
I've got just one precious life to lead,
And I "Thank You," God, for letting me, be me.

Sharon Moore
Ninth Grade - 1978

As an infant in my very first year,
I thought my world was great!
I was fed when I was hungry,
And my meals were seldom late.

My parents laughed and showed me off
When I was only two.
They photographed me day and night
And watched me as I grew.

When I was three, my greatest joy
Was Brush Creek Nursery School.
I loved to play with all the kids,
But sometimes they were cruel!

An older friend scared me to death
When I was four.
She said, ""Real school's awfully hard!"
And I got fears galore.

Kindergarten, after all,
Wasn't quite that bad.
This five-year-old learned how to cope,
And later she was glad.

My family moved when I was six.
To us the house was new.
The oak trees grew around it,
And it had a lovely view.

My brothers built a tree house
When I was only seven.
They actually let me in it once.
I thought I was in heaven!

We got a darling puppy
The year that I was eight.
"Taffy" was the name we gave,
And we thought she was great!

In the year that I was nine,
My cousin, Maggie May,
Flew in from Korea,
And she was here to stay.

When I was ten, I thought ahead
Of how I'd have it made,
Being the "Big Gun" in the school
When I reached sixth grade.

I discovered when eleven
A truth about my fate.
I decide my happiness,
And sixth grade wasn't great!

And now I'm twelve.
I tell the truth,
And I will not pretend
That I am disappointed
That this poem is at an end.

Suzanne Dieter
Seventh Grade - 1981

I was only a baby when I was one,
Another innocent, small face,
Trusting of my mother,
Resting securely in her hold,
But slowly growing curious about my surroundings,
Wondering about what lay beyond the crib.

At two, I discovered the wonders of the household.
A natural prowler was I.
Pots, pans, egg beaters, closets, dressers, tables
Were my new discoveries.
I even dared to venture beyond the kitchen
To discover the new realms of the other rooms.

My first true journey beyond was at three.
All of a sudden my world grew larger.
Trees, leaves, flowers, grass
Came into my grasp and understanding.
I became aware my world was much more,
And more fascinating and strange with every day.

At four, I learned the meaning of school.
I met my teacher and the class.
I'd build with blocks and learn to draw
And jump and spend my time
Trying to learn a nursery rhyme.
That year I think my life was fine.

Airplanes, rockets, jets, and trains
Were my new discovery at five.
My imagination took leaps and bounds,
Bringing me to exotic places.
Suddenly, my world grew immense
With more things for me to discover still.

I got a look at foreign lands
When I turned the age of six.
From the airport away I went
To get a glimpse of the Orient.
I learned to appreciate different ways,
Different customs and other values.

At seven I found a useful weapon.
I learned to use my voice with force.
I'd blast away my parents' ears
To get my way with hurls and tears.
But my life couldn't continue that way.
The time for me to leave was near.

I left to learn new and different ways.
Suddenly, I found a new world.
Ancient cultures, different opportunities
Opened to me suddenly
Like a large door that had been closed
Until I discovered it was there.

I entered into a place of traditions,
Of calm, and peace, and silence at the age of nine.
I met and learned about older values,
The values of discipline and respect,
So hidden to others, I know now
That would soon prove to be a problem.

A ten year old traditional French school boy
Entered into a scatterbrained American school.
Alienation and disaster,
Unprepared to face the changes that took place.

A person of tooth and claw at age eleven
With a tough, thick hide,
Closed in, left out, threatened.
Life was one big struggle.
Treated as if I belonged elsewhere.
"Go back to France where you belong!"
Was all they said to me.

I have learned and adjusted now that I'm twelve.
Life to me is optimistic, exciting, enjoyable.
I look for those who know my world
And hope others will understand.
I've grown in many ways and
Suddenly I feel stronger.

David Jager
Seventh Grade - 1981

Assignment 21 - Word Cinquain

This is a five line poem. The first line is one word. It names a topic. The second line consists of two words which describe and/or define the topic. The third line has three words, each describing action common to the topic. The fourth line (four words) gives your personal opinion about the topic. The fifth line is only one word, and it means the same or nearly the same as the one word first line topic. Write a few and see how easy it is to talk about an idea with a limited number of words.

Time
Forever, endless,
Meticulous, steady, rhythmic.
It will flow on through eternity.
Unlimited.

Bees,
Soft, tiny,
Hovering, plotting, clustering.
One of nature's amazing creations.
Honey.

Jill Joyce
Eighth Grade - 1972

134

People,
Tall, short,
Running, sitting, playing.
Funny things they do.
Humans.

Trash,
Filthy, cluttered,
Stinking, smelling, littering.
Why is it here?
Pollution.

Clouds,
Fluffy, white,
Speeding, wandering, floating.
Ornaments in the sky.
Water.

Doug Grow
Eighth Grade - 1973

Fire
Colorful, hot,
Burning, flickering, destroying.
Campfires feel good.
Flame.

Stars,
Burning, bright,
Orbiting, exploding, mystifying.
Stars give us light.
Novas.

Clay,
Gray, lifeless,
Stretching, shaping, flattening.
I love molding clay.
Art.

Tom Juarez
Seventh Grade - 1977

Kittens,
Soft, furry,
Pounce, play, scurry.
Young cats are energetic.
Cats.

Elephants,
Tall, gray,
Eat, squeal, play.
Elephants are huge animals.
Beasts.

Wars,
Bloody, dark,
Noisy, kill, wound.
Some wars create more.
Battles.

Janeen Reynaud
Seventh Grade - 1977

Water,
Hydrogen, oxygen,
Rushing, splashing, dripping.
Water is very refreshing.
H2O.

Linda Foy
Ninth Grade - 1978

Sadness
Painful, heartbreaking,
Crying grieving, hurting.
Depressing when it's there.
Sorrow.

Air,
Cool, hot,
Blowing, living, mixing.
It keeps the world going.
Oxygen.

136

Rainbows,
Amusing, colorful,
Arching, beautifying, fading.
Interesting to look at.
Arcs.

Cristina Arbunic
Seventh Grade - 1981

Baby,
Small, dependent,
Screaming, crying, sucking!
A miniature human being.
Offspring.

Michelle Sullivan
Seventh Grade - 1981

Assignment 22 - Syllable Cinquain

The syllable cinquain is a five line poem which contains lines of 2, 4, 6, 8, and 2 syllables in that order. This poem should build like a good story from beginning to end.

My nose
Knows the pleasure
Of deeply inhaling
The blossoming flowers in the
Springtime.

Childhood.
I remember
Always being carefree,
Not thinking of anyone else
But me!

Jill Joyce
Eighth Grade - 1972

Homework.
Education.
Learning, thinking, writing.
An illness that teachers give you.
Brainwork.

Humans.

Living beings.
God's greatest creations.
Some good, some bad, some in between.
Mortals.

Cindy L. Polly
Seventh Grade - Student

Poems,
Rhythmic beauty
Sad, happy, funny, strange.
They're a flowing bouquet of words.
Writing.

Tom Juarez
Seventh Grade - 1977

Cheetahs.
They stalk the earth,
Roaming, growling, hunting,
Showing gracefulness in each step.
Magic.

Kelly Boyce
Eighth Grade - 1981

Good friend.
Truthful, helpful.
Makes you feel good inside.
Good to have in times of great need.
Great pal.

Loving,
Warmth, tenderness.
Feels good inside you.
Something you cannot live without.
Caring.

Suzanne Dieter
Seventh Grade - 1981

Assignment 23 - Haiku

As traditionally written by Japanese people for hundreds of years, Haiku usually contained three essential elements: 1) a reference to a season; 2) a feeling; and 3) an implied similarity between two different things. This way of unifying life and embedding it in nature still is a popular short-verse form among Japanese.

The way we Americans write haiku is quite different. We use the same form as the Japanese, i.e., a three line poem of 5, 7, and 5 syllables, respectively, but we pour any kind of an idea we wish into it.

Try writing a few haiku and then rank them from what you consider to be the best to the worst.

The world with its faults
Is still beautiful to me.
It always will be.

Rainbows are beauty.
They create serenity
After a great storm.

A seagull will soar
Just as a feathered sailplane,
Nearly motionless.

Jill Joyce
Eighth Grade - 1972

140

The revolving Earth
Is but a small speck of dust
In the pool of space.

Nature is a gift
That the world can't live without
Even if it tried.

I always find love
In the most unlikely places.
Yet, I still find it.

Doug Grow
Eighth Grade - 1973

Maturing takes time.
Some people never have time
So, they stay the same.

I am myself, me.
I act, look, and feel like me
with no mask or shield.

Janeen Reynaud
Seventh Grade - 1977

The morning dew shines,
Glittering and colorful,
Bringing a new day.

I listened and learned
That nature has its own course,
And I'm included.

The ugly duckling
Lost its childhood feathers.
The beautiful swan.

Linda Foy
Ninth Grade - 1978

The rain was pouring.
It made pattering noises.
I fell asleep.

Suzanne Dieter
Seventh Grade - 1981

Hot dogs and French fries,
The world's two favorite foods,
Meat and potatoes.

Cindy L. Polly
Seventh Grade - 1981

Assignment 24 - Tanka

As originally written, a haiku used to be the first three lines of a five line poem called a tanka. It consisted of lines with 5, 7, 5, 7, 7 syllables. Two people often played a game with this poem. Each would first write a haiku. Then they'd exchange papers, study one another's haiku, and add two seven syllable lines to it. The two line additions extended or changed the thought expressed in the three line haiku.

First, try writing a few tanka by yourself. Then select five to ten of the best haiku you wrote in the previous assignment and exchange them with another student. Cap one another's haiku with two seven syllable lines and return them to see how your partner extended and/or changed your haiku ideas.

A beautiful doll
Has a twinkle in its eye
And returns a smile.
It's a miniature person
To love and hold and cherish.

The beautiful snow
Coming from heaven above
Dances through the sky.
It whirls in maddening fun,
Fearful that soon it will die.

Jill Joyce
Eighth Grade - 1972

A sprawling menace!
Smoke and smog everywhere!
Industry's empire!
Man's sojourn on this fair earth
Is ending in disaster.

Tom Juarez
Seventh Grade - 1977

Love is a feeling
Which comes unnoticed, but grows.
Then blooms and unites,
And two people become one,
Almost starting a new life.

Janeen Reynaud
Seventh Grade - 1977

The trees shook with fear!
A strong wind was blowing hard.
Leaves and branches fell.
Animals ran for shelter.
The storm had hit the island.

Happy animals,
Pink blossoms filling the sky,
Everything blooming,
Everything falling in love!
Spring has finally come around.

Linda Foy
Ninth Grade - 1978

What, really, is time?
Is it the rate life passes?
A thing of the mind?
I doubt it. Because to me,
Time is the meter of life's poem.

Doug Grow
Eighth Grade - 1978

Pink cherry blossoms
Blooming in the spring morning,
Falling to the ground.
Silently floating petals.
Fragrance drifting all around.

Christina Arbunic - 1981

Under the willow,
Beneath the blowing leaves,
I lay quietly,
Thinking of my distant dreams,
Wanting them all to come true.

Kelly Boyce
Eighth Grade - 1981

Scrub vainly brags.
Hawk soars high in majesty.
Mockingbird holds court.
Butterfly floats on the wind,
Content to be who it is.

Suzanne Dieter
Seventh Grade - 1981

Assignment 25 - Korean Sijo (She-Jo)

This verse form is usually about nature (but doesn't have to be when you write it) and has three long lines with fourteen to sixteen syllables in each line. You'll discover that complete stories and explanations can be expressed in three long lines when you write Korean Sijo. Try them; you'll like them!

Animals are truly fascinating and
beautiful things.
Some have feathers; some have scales, fangs,
shells, horns, trunks, beaks, claws, or wings.
Each differs in personality, and a special song
each sings.

Jill Joyce
Eighth Grade - 1972

The wars and inhumane conflicts in which
he participates,
Are disintegrating man's beautiful haven
of life.
I sometimes wonder if man will be able
to survive.

Doug Grow
Eighth Grade- 1973

It was the end of the mile run at the
Rincon Valley Track Meet.
One of the runners, exhausted, was plunging
towards the tape,
When, fast as lightning, another guy passed him
and won the race.

Tom Juarez
Seventh Grade - 1977

Embarrassed? You shouldn't be. That was then, and
this is now.
Don't dwell on the past, but on the future. The future
is your life!
Things change; you change; life changes. Move with
the future; enjoy your ride.

Janeen Reynaud
Seventh Grade - 1977

I danced and danced until my feet felt as if
they'd fall off.
I don't think I'd ever had a better time than
I had that night.
I was doing the one thing I loved with the person
I loved.

The batter walked to the plate with determination
on his face.
The pitch was thrown, and he focused on the
rushing curve ball.
With concentration and strength, he slammed the ball
out of the park.

Linda Foy
Ninth Grade - 1978

Assignment 26 - Diamante

Like the cinquains and tankas, diamantes have five lines. That's where the similarity ends because the diamante I want you to try writing contains nine lines. Diamante means opposite, so, begin your first four lines with thought about a topic like GIRLS, and finish the last four lines with thought about that topic's <u>opposite</u> like BOYS. The <u>fifth</u> or <u>middle line</u> should contain thought about both topics (girls and boys) and provide a smooth <u>transition</u> from one topic to the other. This is just one variation of diamante writing.

Daytime
Is bright,
Clear and cheerful.
Birds sing their songs.
But soon the world darkens.
All becomes quiet, still.
No longer bright.
It is
Night.

Jill Joyce
Eighth Grade - 1972

Light,
Sunny, bright,
Blinding your eyes,
Melting, tanning, burning, fading.
Dimness fades the light away.

Objects are hardly visible
A hidden world,
Cold, mysterious.
Darkness.

Cristina Arbunic
Seventh Grade - 1981

Peace,
Very quiet.
No loud noises.
Air full of happiness.
Very wonderful compared to noise.
Noise is unwanted sounds.
An awful racket.
Very disturbing.
Pollution.

Suzanne Dieter
Seventh Grade - 1981

Life!
Long lasting.
Fulfilling our dreams
With health and happiness.
Life always turns into death.
It waits upon us.
Then it comes.
Forever resting,
Death!

Brendan Kunkle
Seventh Grade - 1981

Assignment 27 - Limerick

Although the essential poetic elements generally consist of an idea, strong feeling, sharp imagery, regular rhythm, and brevity, many poems like <u>limericks add rhyme</u>. Not all limericks are the same.

The limerick you'll write will have five lines. You make the last syllables of lines 1, 2, and 5 rhyme with one another and the last syllables of lines 3 and 4 rhyme with one another. The syllables in each line follow a regular, rhythmical pattern of <u>unaccented</u>, <u>accented</u>, <u>accented</u> syllables. Single syllable words may be used as either accented or unaccented syllables. If you don't know where the accent comes in a word just by hearing it, ask your friendly dictionary for help. Once you catch on to limericking, you won't want to stop because they provide the medium for an awful lot of humor. They can be serious, too. Try a few.

I don't know why there's war,
And I don't know what it's for.
We hope and we pray,
That maybe some day,
'Twill be stopped, not to harm anymore.

I can never hide myself from me,
'Cause I see what others don't see.
But I don't want to run
From the things that I've done,
Just want to be happy and free!

Jill Joyce
Eighth Grade - 1972

There once was a man from L.A.
Who always had nothing to say.
His talk was so boring
He left people snoring,
'Til late in the noontime day.

Brendan Kunkle
Seventh Grade - 1981

There was a young girl from Madrid,
And her bedtime drew near so she hid,
When her father came round,
Found her flat on the ground,
He yelled, "Go to bed!" and she did.

Suzanne Dieter
Seventh Grade - 1981

Assignment 28 - Regular Rhythms

As with the limerick, the beat or rhythm of other poetry is also gotten by selecting words in patterns of <u>accented</u> and <u>unaccented</u> syllables. Four regular rhythmical patterns are: <u>iambic</u> (unaccented-accented); <u>trochaic</u> (accented-unaccented); <u>anapestic</u> (unaccented-unaccented-accented); and <u>dactylic</u> (accented-unaccented-unaccented).

Try writing four different verses, each verse using one of the above rhythm patterns. Use as many lines and rhymes per verse as you wish. When you've finished, try writing a couple of verses with more-or-less regular rhythm that's there just because you feel it's there when you read it back to yourself.

"White and It's Glory"

White is the pearl on
a golden ring;

White is the gaiety of
the songs we sing.

White is the sheet hanging
to dry;

White is the cloud in the
clear, blue sky.

White is the snowflake

on a winter afternoon;

White is the frosting on
a big, wooden spoon.

White is the color of
many a house;

White is the warmth of
a soft, baby mouse.

White is the daintiness of
a wedding gown;

White is the powder on the face
of a clown.

White is our breath on
a winter day;

White is a sailboat
floating away.

Laure Dowdle
Seventh Grade - 1967

"Quick"

Are you disgusted with life?
I'll tell you a wonderful trick.
Do something for somebody,
Quick!

Are you discouraged and tired,
Unhappy, weary, or sick?
Try to make somebody happy,
Quick!

If all the world is dreary,
And clouds are nearing and thick,
Go and try to help someone,
Quick!

The loveliest game of all,
A wonderful one to pick,
Is making others hopeful,
Quick!

Jill Joyce
Eighth Grade - 1972

'Twas midnight in the daytime and summer in the fall.
In the middle of the jungle stood a skyscraper tall.
The roads were jammed with turnips and the stars began to call,
And everywhere you looked you saw a caterpillar stall.

I met a man who could not see
And he described the view to me.

I met a man who could not hear,
Who whistled bird songs in my ear.

I met a man who could not speak.
He told me what I wished to seek.

The score was six to nothing
As Casey joined the huddle.
Before he'd missed a slap shot
And his thoughts were in a muddle.

He threw the ball into the air
And putted on the green.
He dribbled down the backcourt
And looked so very mean.

He aced his serve, he made a goal,
And slid right into home.
That's the story of Casey
And the end of my great poem.

Once upon a noontime dreary
While I wandered weak and weary
Into Rincon Valley's lunchroom, looking for a meal to store,
I encountered people crying, fainting, screaming, barfing, dying,
Students groaning, teachers moaning -- I was praying on the floor.

Orange spaghetti, soggy pizza made my stomach growl and roar.
Would I eat there? Nevermore!

Tom Juarez
Seventh Grade - 1977

Dreams are things that come when you sleep.
They're quiet (not loud), never making a peep.
They keep you alive when you're lying in bed,
Not moving your body, but thoughts in your head.
In dreams you do things you don't do when you're awake,
Like killing people, or even jumping in a lake.
You can't make dreams happen; they come on their own.
But they're always there, for your head is their home.

Have you ever thought back,
At what you used to do?
And wished it had been someone else,
And not you?

Janeen Reynaud
Seventh Grade - 1977

Mom knows corn on the cob is my favorite dish,
And she cooks it on Sunday with chicken and fish.
As for spinach, I hate it! I can't stand the taste!
If it's part of my dinner, it all goes to waste!

Suzanne Dieter
Seventh Grade - 1981

Assignment 29 – Narrative Poem

Two of the main kinds of poetry are lyric and narrative. Lyric poems are short and songlike; narrative poems are long and tell a story. Think of a story you'd like to tell, but instead of using paragraphs for the story parts, use <u>verses</u>. If you finish before the other students, try turning one of your recently read novels into a narrative poem.

The boy walked solemnly down the road,
His thumb in the air,
A red bow in his hair.

He was an average kid,
But of the "cool", "groovy" type.
His thoughts were of peace,
And he shuddered at a fight.

But this boy was young,
Too young to run away.
He would now have
To steal to make his pay.

"The world doesn't love me,
My parents don't understand.
The only way I'll get by,
Is to live off the land."

But the land wasn't livable,
And the city was big.
The air was polluted,

And the water hardly fit for a pig!

"Come with us,"
Said his "hippy" friends.
"We will give you food.
We will give you a place to sleep,
And a home to call your own."

He went their way,
Thus turning to the slums,
For his friends had given him nothing.
He begged and stole,
Finally learning to eat mold,
But his life got worse,
And his future seemed to be cursed.

Again he sought help,
But now of strangers.
"Of course we will help you.
Just one shot of this,
Your troubles are over,
And who knows how many you'll miss?"

So he took the savage needle.
Death was in his hands.
He knew the thing was evil,
It killed men of many lands.

"Let's go, sonny.
There's no time to waste.
Blow your mind!
Take a trip!
It's easy to make cloud nine!"

Yet the boy would not.
Instead, he turned away,
And silently cried
for his worried "Pop."

With feet a-flying,
And tears running free,
The boy thought of home,
Bouncing on Mommy's knee.

"Please, Mr. Policeman!
Take me to 113 Grove,
For you see, I'm scared,
And I want to go home!"

In a matter of minutes,
He hugged his mother tightly,
Tears of joy, happiness, and glee.
For this young boy would never again
Walk solemnly down the road.

Daryl Nelson
Seventh Grade - 1969

Narrative Poem: A translation of the anonymously authored diary, Go Ask Alice.

"It Happened to Alice"

Alice was a warm, happy person.
She kept a diary which contained her every thought, every emotion.

She moved away from a favorite place and familiar friends,
To a place strange and unknown.

She took the role of a wallflower,
Every lonely moment at school
Wanting so much to be in with a group,
To fit in anywhere.

People change,
Sometimes overnight,
Over the summer.
Alice did!

She tried drugs,
But was a victim,
Of a gag? A joke?
No one really knew,
Not even Alice.
She wanted to fit in.
Thought it was wild,
Just a fun kick,

Swearing never to do it again.

She couldn't resist,
And did it again.
Now she was almost in another world,
One completely different,
But exciting to her.

She began to neglect her appearance,
Her language, and family.
She had really changed.

After awhile,
Getting tired of the hassle and the mess,
She took a risky, wide, gaping step
Trying to get to the other side,
But the rules of society pushed her back, and
She got caught in between that dangerous step.

She was so mixed up, and
She had no one to turn to.
She had taken a chance
But didn't succeed.
No one would accept her.
She was lost!

Her old life style gradually came back to her,
Her happy nature,
Because she had found someone,
Someone she could trust and confide in.
She loved him!

But suddenly Alice
Died of an overdose!
Yes, it was unexplainable.
No one could say why.

It just happened!
It happened to Alice.

Cory Deibert
Eighth Grade - 1974

Assignment 30 – Sonnet

A sonnet is a <u>lyric poem</u> which expresses strong personal emotion. The two kinds of sonnets you'll try are the Shakespearean and the Italian. One of each will be plenty.

First the requirements for the <u>Shakespearean</u> sonnet:

1) 14 lines

2) Each line contains 10 syllables.

3) The syllables must follow an <u>iambic</u> rhythm pattern (unaccented-accented).

4) The rhyme scheme is abab cdcd efef gg.

In the <u>Italian</u> sonnet, the first eight lines state a theme or experience, and the last six respond to or comment on the theme. Otherwise, its requirements are the same as the Shakespearean sonnet, except for the rhyme schemes which can be either abba abba cdcdcd or abba abba cde cde.

> To love, to laugh, to play the game of life,
> Each man alive seeks to survive at least,
> Through one life's span to rise above the strife
> That each day brings between the times of feast.
>
> The feast is love, a giving kind that must
> Be shared to be enjoyed. The giver takes all.

The game goes to the stronger man if just
He never looks for gain in love at all.

His soul and all his life are spent in search
Of why we're born and why we die and how
We span the time between like swaying birch,
Wind-bent and battered, uprooted and forced to bow.

But always the hope that the pain will be shared by one other
Who loves you as deeply as a lover or parents or brother.

Cory Antipa
Ninth Grade - 1967

Where is the wonder that I once believed
Watching snowflakes melt as a child?
Where is the wonder that had me deceived
When a mountain of blue and green turns wild?

Where's the magic that thrilled my heart abold
Watching the flowers growing in the spring?
Where is the magic that filled the sky gold?
How did the robins know to fly and sing?

Where are the mysteries that I couldn't solve?
What could have changed a kitten to a bat?
What made the world understand to revolve?
Why couldn't we be grateful just like that?

What is it a child can feel now and then?
Where's the wonder I'll never know again?

Denise Howard
Ninth Grade - 1967

There still exists on this most wretched Earth
Those wayward deeds of man we know as crime,
That lead the weak of high and lowly birth
Down paths of gloomy muck and mire and slime.

Conceived in hopes that warped and went askew,
The wicked seed doth grow in rankest greed
To fruit that poisons now as hitherto,

And which doth cause the hardest heart to bleed.

A fruit so bitter as to bite the tongue,
To hurt the soul and make the throat constrict.
By such folly are all good values flung,
Dreams of happiness broken, pricked.

The gains of crime that beckon or inspire
Are not worth the scathing burns of hell's fire!

Michael Sims
Ninth Grade - 1967

Italian Sonnet

"If"

If all the world would fight to keep some peace,
Instead of taking one another's side.
If all the world could just forget their pride,
Then maybe all our days at war would cease.

If all the countries could enforce a lease,
Agreeing that our peace would be world-wide,
And all attempts of war would be denied,
Our chance of killing war would soon increase.

Then maybe it would not go on for long,
And who knows what disaster war might bring,
For every day our weapons get more strong,
Enabling us to do most anything.
If we destroy our earth, it would be wrong.
Of our stupidity the sky would ring.

Jill Joyce
Eighth Grade - 1972

"The Ocean"

The crisp breeze felt cool blowing at my face.
The odor of salt water stained the air,

And being there freed me from the rat race.
I didn't worry then and didn't care.

I lived, what life was left to live, in peace.
The sea brought comfort in its own strange way.
Tides that splashed upon the pier never ceased.
Sea shells rested on damp sand in bright array.

High waves, like clawing fingers, grasped the beach.
When the warm waves rolled in, they filled my heart
And brought back memories that were hard to reach.
This time my feelings were not torn apart.

The great warmth of this ocean was like me.
It seemed to fight for its right to be free.

Melanie Solie
Seventh Grade - 1975

"Tennis"

He smashed the ball -- it whizzed across the net.
As it came close, I heard it make a hum.
I thought my forehand was my safest bet,
But it went past, and I felt really dumb.

The score was thirty love, and I was sore.
(Why did I ever get into this sport?)
He served again, much faster than before.
I hit it, but it flew out of the court.

He double faulted; it was forty-five.
My next return went whistling past his ear.
Another double fault! I must survive.
"The score is deuce!" His voice shook with fear.

And then, "Add out," swat, and it was "Game!"
I'd made it to the Tennis Hall of Fame!

Tom Juarez
Seventh Grade 1977

163

Assignment 31 - Free Verse

You're free at last! No rhyme or rhythm is needed to write this kind of poetry. What is needed is a strong and deep "feeling" for what you're trying to say, and after you've done your best and said it, let it go at that. Spoken English is naturally a very musical language, and you'll find that the more "feeling" you put into your speech, the more poetic it becomes naturally. Free verse sits on the dividing line between prose and poetry. Pick your "feeling" and write to your heart's content.

"Life"

You have to hold life
With the touch of a child
When the words of your heart are its tears
Seek strength in the learned
Hope in the loved
And truth as your slayer of fears.

You have to cry out
Though your voice may be muffled
Bound by the mask that you wear
Lean on the faithful
Take refuge in trust
And be open to those who care.

You have to believe
Though your dreams have been shattered
And pain lines the edge of your soul

Alone you are worthy
As one you are loved
All the pieces of you make a whole.

You have to accept
There are thorns with the roses
And even the strong can be weak
Stand tall to your merit
Be faithless to shame
Make it freedom from guilt that you seek.

You have to forgive
Hatred strangles a bond
Don't send off your anguish to war
Seek peace in the battle
And cherish the past
For killed love will not settle the score.

You have to forge on
Through the arduous journey
Though your spirit grows weak in the night
Look to the stars
And call faith as your guide
With God as your beacon of light.

You have to keep searching
When all seems for naught
And your heart pleads a reason for living
Betray your self pity
And tend to the world
For there's strength to be had in the giving.

So hold onto life
With the touch of a child
Believe that there's always a way
Live for the moment
Remember to dream
And find peace in the dawn of the day.

Patricia Dowdle
Ninth Grade - 1971

"Pollution"

The cars zoom by,
The fast, the slow, new and old.
Don't they know they're all gonna die?
This whole world is beginning to mold.

Factories spit their filthy smoke into the air,
Adding to the smoke in the sky.
What's wrong with them, don't they care?
They're watching it all pass by.

Fish that used to swim the cool, clear water
Have been swallowed up by the dirt.
The mother fish probably never lives to see her son or daughter,
But what do we care, the fish are the ones getting hurt.

The government is working on it.
The establishment is considering it.
Are today's youth ignoring it?

What can I do?
I'm only a kid.
Pretty soon my life will be through,
But what can I say I did?

Don't worry. We'll be all right.
Pretty soon they'll see the light.

Debbie Bagala
Eighth Grade 1970

Dream, wish, hope.
God, I've been a dope!
I've reached the end of my rope.

I'm going down, down.
I hope I'm never found.
I've got to leave this town,
My head is spinning round.

I'm surrounded by a pool of tears,

Trying to hide from my fears.
I've cried and I've tried,
And now I feel as though I've died.

Summer is drawing near,
And I've got to figure this whole thing out.
I'll try to be sincere,
But I don't think I can do without.

He knows I like him,
And he shows me his hate.
Is he putting on a show,
Or is this my fate?

He has a reputation to uphold.
Maybe that's why he's been so cold.

Debbie Bagala
Eighth Grade - 1970

No walls can hold off its force.
No lecture can make it any weaker.
No law can prohibit it.
No key can lock it in a closet.
Love penetrates through the darkness of time.

Carole Chudwick
Eighth Grade - 1970

How beautiful is nature
As it spreads before my eyes,
Its glorious green plants,
Its animals running free.
How beautiful is nature
With the uniqueness of each creature,
Each creature a separate life,
Life to be cherished,
Birth, then death,
Seed, then withered plant.
But life has unfolded during the hours.
Life.

How beautiful is nature.
How beautiful is life.

Carole Chudwick
Eighth Grade - 1970

Watch a river flow to the sea,
Watch a river flow past me,
Endless journey to a gathering place.
All rivers, creeks, congregate,
Mixing their waters until all is one,
Working together under the sun.

Why can't people meet at one place?
Even though different, unite?
Why can't people have a common race,
Or at least think as one?
Rivers flow, people argue.
The river has a destination.
Do we, my friend?

Carole Chudwick
Eighth Grade - 1970

I saw a man walking on a freeway banking,
Backpack securely tied in place,
Flute held lovingly in his hands,
Held to his lips, making mellow music.
He walked with easy flowing steps
As if behind him were many miles already walked.
His hair blew freely in the wind,
Free enough to dangle where it pleased.
And as I watched him go his way,
While we went another,
My companion looked on yearningly, saying,
"I wonder where's he's going."
And I knew he wanted to go with him,
With his backpack and his harmonica,
And his thumb to ride on.
We drove past,
Leaving part of our beings

With the wanderer
Who travels across the country
Finding what's before him.
Wanderers like this fluted knight
Dot the country - the world.

Carole Chudwick
Eighth Grade - 1970

A child's first years of school they say
Are his best and his funnest every day.
He can spend his day in a nice, cute class,
Reading and thinking of questions to ask.
He can play or talk when 'er he wants,
And the teacher he can always haunt.
He can learn his lessons in such a way
He can hardly wait for school each day.

Well, this is what the A-dults say,
But many children feel not this way.
They feel that school's a place to go,
Where the teacher can preach all he might know,
And that really it's just a place for some
To be rid from the house their very young.

It's a place to make a person feel bad
When their friends get better grades than they had,
And a good excuse for parents to scold
When their child does other than the assignments told.
It's a time when children see if they're accepted
For their toys, themselves, or doing what's expected.
And a time when if you haven't a friend
You're alone every minute from morning to end.

This is how it always seems,
And little to children it really means.
But I guess it is good in one special way.
Children learn they can't do what they want every day,
And they learn to appreciate holidays more.
But is this what school is really for?

Linda Escola
Seventh Grade - 1970

This poem is to be read fast and desperately, preferably in three breaths.

Hassle, Fight, Stab!
Who wears the nicest things?
Who throws the wildest parties?
Who makes out?
Who takes pot?
Who has the friends?
Who has money?
Who got busted?
Hypocrites! I scream in all my arrogant omnipotence,
No better than those I scream at.
Belong!
Get with it!
Get in!
You haven't time to waste;
The rats have started running.
Live!
The world is sinking fast.
You haven't time to waste.
Dance!
Yell!
Do wild things to be regretted!
Get married young!
It don't make no difference when you do it.
It never works nohow.
Kiss the shadows of the past Farewell.
They are gone, so sings the knell.
Death and life so transcendental,
Of no importance.
How could they be, they are so easy come by.
The Gods sit on their chaise lounges,
Spitting grape seeds at their creations!
Mankind doesn't own the world;
They rented it from God.
The deed is being torn.
We sit on earth in the wastes of our existence
And hide behind the shield of our illusion,
Pretending we simply cannot die.

The Gods sit on their chaise lounges
And spit cherry pits at us!
Man sits in crowded cities,
Existing, not living.
Producing children out of boredom,
Sentencing to fight the fight we fought and lost.

Beware,

the

Gods are eating avocadoes!

Kim Haylock
Eighth Grade - 1970

If man would try harder to get along with others,
If he would lend a hand instead of criticize,
If deep in his heart he would love his brothers,
Then this to me would mean that man was finally getting wise.
It is said that man is wise, but I do not believe it.
Why would a wise man continue to kill off his species?
If a man fails, he still continues to strike and hit
Until he gets his way,
And then he finally sees that for him to reach the top,
He has put others down.
If everyone could have a chance to live his own way,
Instead of being told what to do by someone on a higher mound,
If everything, no matter how small, could have a chance to say
Where it wanted to live, and why,
If everything wasn't run by a computer,
And man could once more see the beautiful, blue sky,
If everyone on this earth could have God as his tutor,
Then man would see that love and peace are
The only things worth living for.

Randy Ryan
Eighth Grade - 1970

Mom,
You are a flower in the garden of life.
I view you in quiet solitude . . .

Unaware that I, too, am being watched.

You glisten before me,
Moistened with the dew of concern,
Yet shining brilliantly with the glow of success.

You have built a strong path for me,
And I, by your guidance and love,
Have grown and matured along the way.

We both know that I am still a young seed.
I cannot plant myself in your garden,
Nor stay quietly by your side.
I must leave in search of material
With which I will build my own path . . . my own life.

You love and are loved.
By your love I shall blossom.

All my love,

Patty

Patricia Dowdle
Ninth Grade - 1971

Dad,
Where there is life -- there is meaning.
Where there is compassion -- there is peace.
Where there is light -- there is hope.
Where there is optimism -- there is happiness.
Where there is love -- there is you.
To merely exist is one thing.
To be remembered as the most wonderful father
That a girl could ever want
For so many beautiful reasons
Is quite another.

Thank you for the love which has made my life so happy.

Love,
Pat

Patricia Dowdle
Ninth Grade - 1971

Love someone not only for what they are,
But for what you are when you're with them.
Love not only for what they make of themselves,
But for what they make of you.
Love them for the part of you they bring out.
Love them because they do more than anyone else could.
Love them because with them you can be yourself.

Jill Joyce
Eighth Grade - 1972

"And Then?"

You have an ambition and a goal,
And then you achieve both and work hard and honestly.
And then you settle your home,
And then you start your children with the same opportunity.
And then you have a peaceful old age.
And then you die.
And then?

Jill Joyce
Eighth Grade - 1972

At times when life is drab, and you feel bad,
It helps to sit and think of cheery things.

A rainbow's truthful promise after rain,
The morning's gold that shines in through your door.

A dandelion puff that you can blow,
The clear and trickling brooks that always run.

Just think of all the fluffy things in life,
To hold and cuddle, squeeze and love and see.

A field of daisies blowing in the wind,
A bed of roses lightening your heart.

173

The stars that you can wish on every night.
Things aren't so bad if you learn how to dream.

Jill Joyce
Eighth Grade - 1972

"How To Fit In"

How to fit in!
That's what I'd like to know.
Should I cut my hair short
Or wear the right clothes?
Who's the big put on for!
Heaven only knows.

How to fit in!
What's the big deal?
Don't buy your clothes.
Just go out and steal!
You're judged by the way ya act,
Not by the way you feel.

You can smoke your pot
And take your pills!
You can do your thing and
Get your thrills!
But me, I'll just ask myself
Again and again,
"Why can't I be me,
Yet still fit in?"

Laura Christensen
Seventh Grade - 1975

Hold on! Don't let go. You can hold on.
Don't explode!
The pressure will ease off, and it will
All work out.
Don't you do something you will regret later.

Janeen Reynaud
Seventh Grade - 1977

"A One-Sided Love Affair"

He has changed my life from dying dogs to singing birds.
It's oh, so beautiful, though everything is unspoken words.

It's a one-sided love affair; he only wants to be a friend.
Yet I continue to fantasize, being unable to face the end.

The end of what? I say, there never was even a start.
Oh, how I wish I could win his heart!

I'll never give up trying; no, I'll never ever quit.
Sooner or later he'll take to me, even if it takes all my wit!

"To Watch the Moon So Silently"

The stars were alone last night.
There was no romanticism in their light,
For my lover had left me.
He said he intended to be free.
And then I watched the moon so silently.

Yes, my life was ruined last night.
I now live my life in fright
Because I know there will never be
Another Cupid, that is, in reality,
And now I watch the moon so silently.

I know someday I must learn
To cope with a first degree burn,
Because there will never be another we,
Just another irresponsible me
To watch the moon so silently.

Linda Foy
Ninth Grade - 1978

"Rejected Again"

Don't cut me down!
Just leave me alone!
You are so popular,

175

And I'm so unknown.
Why don't you help me
Instead of turning me away?
Why don't you accept me?
Oh, I guess that'd be the day.
Hey, people! I'm alive!
Just like you!
I may not be as good,
But I wanna be loved, too!

Linda Jennings
Ninth Grade - 1978

"Heart Broken"

The girl's heart was empty.
A pang of loneliness shot through her.
She felt neglected and rejected.
But she would soon overcome her grieving sorrow,
And see the light of tomorrow.

Cristina Arbunic
Seventh Grade - 1981

Flowers blossom everywhere.
They are ever so beautiful that they leave us reeling.
The girls all wear them in their hair.
They fill our lives with beauty and feeling.

Some people called him a coward,
But I knew he wouldn't run from fears.
I knew he was really a man.

Brendan Kunkle
Seventh Grade - 1981